WHAT PEOPLE ARE SAYING ABOUT ANDREW TOWE AND *BREAKING THE SPIRIT OF DELILAH*...

Every believer has faced moments of spiritual attack. It is impossible to navigate life and destiny without facing demonic opposition. Sadly, some people have chosen the ineffective "ostrich method" of burying their head in the sand and hoping the devil will just go away! This is silly and a waste of time. The enemy must be discerned, confronted, and expelled with authority!

"Lest Satan should get an advantage of us: for we are not ignorant of his devices" (2 Corinthians 2:11). Satan seeks to gain advantage over the people of God by hiding under the cover of darkness. Prophetic voices uncover and unveil hidden demons and demonic plots. In this insightful book, Andrew Towe peels back the cover and reveals a scheming spirit that comes to lull the people of God to sleep. Some of you will read these pages and receive an awakening as you discern what has been hindering you. This reality, in and of itself, makes this book worth reading. But there is more!

You will also be given insight and strategy to overcome the attacks of the enemy. This book is a prophetic wake-up call for the church and believers. It arms us with a prophetic road map to maximize our purpose. So, get ready for a phenomenal journey. Grab a good cup of coffee or another beverage of choice and dive deep into the prophetic brilliance captured in this masterful writing by Andrew, who is a part of my spiritual family and a seasoned leader in the body of Christ! Enjoy.

—*Ryan LeStrange*
Author, *Breaking Curses* and *Hell's Toxic Trio*

T0003993

My friend Andrew Towe is very serious about helping people receive their complete deliverance from every enemy assignment that has tried to assassinate their destiny. His latest book, *Breaking the Spirit of Delilah*, provides spiritual keys and practical tools for dealing with this wicked and demonic spirit. If you've been caught up in the enemy's lies, trapped within the bondage of vicious cycles, and feeling hopeless, it's time to get free! Read this book, follow its biblical advice, and advance into the victorious life that Jesus has promised you can live!

—*Joshua Mills*
Director and co-founder, International Glory Ministries
Best-selling author, *Power Portals* and *Angelic Activations*

Andrew Towe has masterfully compiled revelation and information to help the church identify its blind side. We must operate in the highest and greatest anointing now more than ever before. Jesus is coming soon, and He needs His people fully armed and fully aware. Be equipped as you read *Breaking the Spirit of Delilah*.

—*Kim Owens*
Revivalist; co-pastor, Fresh Start Church, Peoria, AZ
Author, *Doorkeepers of Revival*

Breaking the Spirit of Delilah is a book that will awaken the body of Christ and sound the alarm to the insidious plot that strangles the move of God and strips believers of their power, identity, prophetic purpose, and assignment. In this one-of-a-kind book, Andrew Towe, an apostolic and prophetic leader, enlightens, equips, and encourages every believer to rise up in power and authority. *Breaking the Spirit of Delilah* will open your spiritual eyes to the seducing, deceiving, manipulating, cunning, and tormenting spirit that attacks the work of God. This life-changing book is full of sound biblical teaching, revelation, prophetic insight, and experiences that connect the reader to keys of identifying and demolishing the strongholds of this devious, mischief-making, and anointing-zapping spirit. For many years, I have read books on the spirits of Jezebel, Python, and Leviathan but none on the Delilah spirit. Andrew Towe has presented a game-changer that arms the church to disarm the constricting powers working behind the spirit of Delilah. I highly endorse and recommend the anointing pages of this deliverance handbook. You will not be able to put it down because you will very quickly be able to discern when, what, why, and how this spirit is in operation, and you will have the Holy Spirit's power to break its chokehold!

—*Dr. Hakeem Collins*
International speaker; founder, Hakeem Collins Ministries
Best-selling author, *Unseen Warfare* and
The Power of Aligning Your Words to God's Will

Now, more than ever, the church needs courage to rise up! War and rumors of war are all around us, and so many of us have grown tired, apathetic, and weary of the days ahead. We were created for more! We are anointed and equipped to take ground for the kingdom. Spiritual warfare is real, and we need to be aware of what's happening around us. Andrew Towe's new book *Breaking the Spirit of Delilah* will not only uncover the mystery behind spiritual apathy but will give us insights to be overcomers who take back what the enemy has stolen!

—*Parker and Jessi Green*
Revivalists, Saturate Global
Best-selling authors, *Wildfires* and *Way of the Violent*

My good friend Andrew Towe has written another powerful, must-read book. Far too many people are pulled away from their assignment and calling by the Delilah spirit. This topic is so important for today because when you start operating in your God-given gift, the spirit of Delilah will try to manipulate you, exactly as it happened to Samson. Many lose focus and stop following the leading of the Holy Spirit when the Delilah spirit attempts to pull them away by the lust of the natural realm.

Every one of us has a breathtaking calling and purpose from God that the enemy wants to stop. This is why I quote Matthew 6:10 a lot: "*Your kingdom come, your will be done, on earth as it is in heaven*" (NIV). Books like this one that expose the different tactics of the enemy are so important. The revelation Andrew unpacks in this book will help you to be on guard in the spirit and defeat the spirit of Delilah when it is unleashed against you. When you are under attack, or whether it's your family and friends that the devil is targeting, this is the book that will help you step into victory.

—Joe Joe Dawson
Apostle, Roar Church Texarkana
Author, *Kingdom Thinking*

I love this book! Andrew Towe's *Breaking the Spirit of Delilah* contains many interesting thoughts and valuable insights from Scripture that I have meditated on for decades. It contains a thoughtful critique and a powerful spiritual antidote for the many modern ministry philosophies that emphasize people-pleasing techniques for the masses while de-emphasizing the power of the Holy Spirit. It provides many practical insights and relevant biblical applications for dealing with the kind of lukewarm, non-supernatural, or even anti-supernatural worldviews that the enemy uses to keep God's people in a place of bondage and blindness, while preventing them from entering into the destiny He always intended them to experience.

—Joan Hunter
Evangelist; host, *Miracles Happen!* TV show
Author, *The Power of Prophetic Vision* and *Nine Plus*

Upon my initial reading of Andrew Towe's latest book, the title immediately caught my attention: *Breaking the Spirit of Delilah*. As I perused its pages, I quickly realized that Delilah was not only after me but after you, too! I truly believe that this author has received this revelation directly from the throne room of heaven! The Lord gave me insight on this malevolent spirit that specifically targets the saints of God. Its job is to wear out believers. This spirit launches sneak attacks when Christians are at their most vulnerable, with the objective of lulling them to sleep even while they appear awake.

The spirit of Delilah, as described by the author, sheds light on what has been holding many people hostage for years. Towe exposes and expounds on the various stratagems that Delilah utilizes to keep believers trapped in a stranglehold of slumbering. This spirit desires to initiate, maintain, prolong, and exacerbate supernatural lassitude (weariness). Perhaps this was the same spirit that caused Moses to experience an inexplicable exhaustion while Israel battled the Amalekites in Exodus 17. I was extremely impressed by the transparency, compassion, and authenticity of the author.

Andrew Towe has sounded a reverberating prophetic alarm that will most definitely awaken the anointed and the called. There is definitely oil on this book! I believe that after you read *Breaking the Spirit of Delilah*, an increased hunger for the things of God will overtake you. This book is a spiritual wake-up call to "oily" people that Delilah is attempting to trick into slumber. It will be a welcome addition to your spiritual library.

—*John Veal*
Prophet, Enduring Faith Christian Center
Author, *Supernaturally Prophetic*
and *Supernaturally Delivered*

Andrew Towe's *Breaking the Spirit of Delilah* is a must-read for everyone in the church. This book exposes one of the most subtle spirits that has slithered its way into the modern-day church by injecting its venom and putting a slumbering stranglehold on many highly anointed saints of God. This spirit is known as the Delilah spirit. Yes, Delilah was a woman; however, there was a spirit operating through seduction, deception, and manipulation to weaken Samson to find out the source of his strength. That same spirit is operating today in our churches to weaken us as believers and cause us to give up and throw in the towel. We must refuse to allow Delilah to administer her poisonous anesthetic to us.

In this book, you will learn how to recognize the Delilah spirit and identify the spiritual symptoms that come from it. You will also learn how to stop it from stealing your destiny as you discover how to take hold of the keys that will bring you overall victory!

—*Donna Grisham*
Founder and president, Journeys of Choice
Author, *Journeys of Choice*
Host, *The Real Pro-Choice*

BREAKING THE
SPIRIT
OF
DELILAH

ANDREW TOWE

BREAKING THE
SPIRIT
OF
DELILAH

ACCESSING GOD'S POWER
TO TOPPLE ANCIENT STRONGHOLDS

WHITAKER
HOUSE

BREAKING THE SPIRIT OF DELILAH:
Accessing God's Power to Topple Ancient Strongholds

andrewtowe.org
andrew.towe@theramp.org

ISBN: 978-1-64123-947-9 • eBook ISBN: 978-1-64123-948-6
Printed in Colombia
© 2023 by Andrew Towe

Whitaker House • 1030 Hunt Valley Circle • New Kensington, PA 15068
www.whitakerhouse.com

Library of Congress Cataloging-in-Publication Data (Pending)

1 2 3 4 5 6 7 8 9 10 11 ᴜᴜ 30 29 28 27 26 25 24 23

CONTENTS

FOREWORD

For decades, the body of Christ has learned details concerning what ministers identified as a "Jezebel spirit." However, over the past several years, there has been a release of another type of spirit that actually attacks on a more *individual* level. This is the Delilah spirit.

In the New Testament, Jude tells us that believers should contend for the faith and not follow the destructive patterns of three men: Cain, Korah, and Balaam. Cain became enraged with jealousy, slaying his brother over an offering. Korah led a rebellion against spiritual authority, desiring a position that God refused him. Balaam was a compromiser who was willing to merchandise his prophetic gift for personal gain.

The Delilah spirit is more than a seducing spirit. This spirit can spot and capitalize on a person's weakness. It plays with your emotions and your thoughts. It attracts you to things that will eventually bring about your destruction. The detailed, concealed nuggets in the story of Samson and his seductress, Delilah, reveal the very methods this spirit uses to seduce you into a state of depression and defeat.

Once again, pastor, teacher, and author Andrew Towe has done a remarkable job of unmasking this spirit that is presently on a rampage, seeking whom it may devour. This spirit works slowly and is often so crafty that it remains undetected—to the point that an individual can become familiar and comfortable around a person who is operating under the spell and influence of this spirit.

This revelation is one of the most important, as it relates to the times and seasons we have entered. This is more than a book or a great study. It is a spiritual warfare manual. If followed, it could help you to keep your eyesight (your understanding), your anointing, and your calling under God's protective covering.

—*Perry Stone Jr.*
Founder, Voice of Evangelism Outreach Ministries (VOE)

ACKNOWLEDGMENTS

No words could accurately convey my love and appreciation for my wife, Brooke. You have been my biggest cheerleader, encourager, best friend, mother of my children, co-pastor, and wife. I will never forget the service when we started our ministry; no one other than you came. I wanted to leave and forget the service. But, you pointed your finger at me and said, "Andrew Towe, you are called of God to preach. Get behind that pulpit and preach! God sees you being faithful, and I will not let you quit." Thank you for not letting me quit. God definitely knew what He was doing when He gave me you.

Giuliana and Gabriel, you both are our miracle babies. When the doctors said, "No," God said, "Yes." All of the wonderful prophecies that we stood on, believing for you, pale compared to the wonderful gifts you are to us. God always exceeds His promises. Never forget that you have been marked and set apart by God to be world changers! Daddy loves you both so much.

I want to acknowledge my mother, Dr. Carol Elaine, and my stepfather, Scott. Thank you for making Jesus irresistible. You allowed me to sing in your services as a child and taught me the importance of the anointing. Mom, you believed in this book and pressed me to write it. You spent countless hours reading through my writing, editing the contents, and teaching me how to become a better writer. Your knowledge of the Word still amazes me. I love you both.

Thank you to my dad, Rick Towe, and my stepmother, Karen, for constantly pushing me out of my comfort zone and stretching me to run further. You have advised, supported, and encouraged me. Your strength, character, and passion for awakening are changing a generation. Thank you for always being real in God and blazing the trail for me to follow.

A special thanks to my sister, Autumn, and my brother-in-law, Eric, who have been two of my biggest supporters from the very beginning and some of my closest friends. I love you both.

To my in-laws, Rick and Faye Genter—your love and support mean the world to me.

Thank you to all of the Ramp Church family, staff, and intercessors for your prayers, encouragement, and support. You have fought by my side in the trenches and helped me sound the alarm to awaken champions from the lap of Delilah.

To my spiritual sons and daughters, I love you. I am honored to nurture, correct, train, and equip you. You all are definitely *agents of awakening*!

A special thanks to all the pastors, conference hosts, and media ministries who have allowed me to be their guest and trusted me with their platforms to declare the Word of the Lord.

I would like to acknowledge Steve Shultz and the Elijah List. Thank you for being faithful to give a place for the prophets to release the heart of God, for being humble and stewarding what He has trusted you with grace and humility.

I want to give special recognition to apostles Ryan and Joy LeStrange: thank you for pouring into me. You have always challenged me to build higher and stronger.

My heartfelt thanks to Don Milam for believing in this author and to Christine Whitaker and all of the team at Whitaker House for giving me the platform to publish the prophetic Word of the Lord.

INTRODUCTION

Are you experiencing a lack of passion for the presence of God? Are confusing and tormenting thoughts plaguing your mind? Do you feel like giving up because the battle has been so fierce? Then you are almost certainly under attack by the spirit of Delilah.

Although Delilah the woman, whose story we read in the book of Judges, was flesh and blood, beneath the surface, an evil force controlled her to bring down one of the mightiest warriors of the Bible, Samson. The demonic spirit that possessed her is still operating in the world today. I believe that this demonic spirit has taken supremacy over all other wicked spirits at this hour—Jezebel, Python, Leviathan—due to the current spiritual, political, economic, and physiological climate of today's world. The Delilah spirit has maneuvered itself into a position within the modern church, seeking to place its slumber-inducing stranglehold on many of God's highly anointed, chosen, and called saints. Its agenda is to stop believers from fulfilling their divine destiny.

Take note that this spirit does not go after unbelievers. Yes, you read that right! Hell has given this spirit a mission to hunt and track down sons and daughters of the Most High whom He has set apart for Himself for this last hour. Its agenda is to rob them of their strength and devastate their purpose in life. This spirit has no interest in the passive and passionless Christian. Its assignment is to shipwreck the faith and work of those who love God and are actively involved in the work of His kingdom. It seduces, entices, berates, and causes even the strongest of Christians to fall asleep while it works in secret for Satan to gain an advantage over God's people.

This book was written to expose the Delilah spirit and blast the prophetic trumpet of awakening to all believers—including you.

A CHURCH UNDER ATTACK

Whether you realize it or not, you have probably been exposed to the Delilah spirit's hellish directives. Unless you are equipped to recognize its deadly web of enticement, you aren't likely to pick up your weapon and fight against it. God has made a way, through His Son, Jesus, for you to live in freedom from every plot of the enemy. Child of God, you have authority through the name of Jesus over every demonic entity.

The apostle Paul warned us that this deceiving spirit would indeed rise again to strike out against the body of Christ:

> *This know also, that in the last days perilous times shall come. For men shall be lovers of their own selves, covetous, boasters, proud, blasphemers, disobedient to parents, unthankful, unholy, without natural affection, trucebreakers, false accusers, incontinent, fierce, despisers of those that are good, traitors, heady, high-minded, lovers of pleasures more than lovers of God; having a form of godliness, but denying the power thereof: from such turn away.* (2 Timothy 3:1–5)

The spirit of Delilah causes God's people to set aside their genuine hunger for God's presence and instead settle for *"having a form of godliness, but denying the power thereof."* This means disallowing the gifts of the Holy Spirit, rebuffing holy living, mistakenly categorizing holiness as a religious spirit, and replacing God's presence with cheap and powerless substitutions. Satan laughs with glee when believers, who have been given all power and authority over all the works of the devil, attend a social-club-type church and live a compromised life. He loves it when the children of God lose their zeal to rise up and bind him. Satan fears the manifestation of God's sons and daughters and actively seeks to put them to sleep so that he can zap them of their strength.

The spirit that operated in the woman Delilah was one of seduction, deception, manipulation, torment, and accusation. The demonic spirit of Delilah is working overtime to seduce and deceive the church in this hour. Its deepest desire is for you to lay your head in its lap so that it may lull you to sleep. Its craving is for believers to jeopardize their anointing and come under the risk of destruction.

My purpose in writing this book is to expose this devious spirit that has taken hold of the blood-bought church of the living God. Every line of each chapter will uncover Delilah's wicked deceptions that have compromised many of God's chosen vessels. We will look more closely into the mission of the spirit of Delilah, which is to lure believers into a state of weakness and slumber, thereby robbing them of their power. You will understand how to live awakened and revived, and to enthrone Jesus in His rightful place as the Lord of His church.

ARISE!

There is a move of revival coming unlike any this world has ever experienced. Nowhere in the New Testament do you find the apostles "watering down" or attempting to make the gospel of

Jesus Christ palatable for everyone. No, they refused to compromise; they refused to stop preaching in the name of Jesus, even after being threatened, beaten, and imprisoned. Instead, the radical New Testament church moved forward, confirming the good news of Jesus Christ that they proclaimed with miracles, signs, and wonders.

We are God's church. We have been chosen to partner with the Holy Spirit in transforming lives, communities, cities, regions, nations, and generations for Jesus. You and I are ambassadors for His kingdom.

The original victim of the Delilah spirit, Samson, too, had a special purpose: he was called to be a deliverer of the Israelites, God's people. Sadly, Samson fell prey to a deceptive, predatory, slumber-inducing spirit. Much of the church, too, has gone to sleep and forfeited its authority of power as the church to defeat the enemy.

We can't afford to fall asleep! God wants us to realize that we have been given the keys of heaven.

I will give you the keys of heaven's kingdom realm to forbid on earth that which is forbidden in heaven, and to release on earth that which is released in heaven. (Matthew 16:19 TPT)

Keys are a symbol of authority. The ones who carry the keys have been granted permission to unlock and provide entry to that which has been locked up. You have access to release heaven to earth. God desires to use *you*. This is the hour for you to arise, walk in authority, and take dominion over the enemy.

The Lord has commissioned me to write this book to allow His words to roar the sound of awakening to each and every believer. Within the pages of this book is revelation that will stop the spirit of Delilah in its tracks and free you from its evil clutches.

The spirit that operated through the woman Delilah attacked Samson's mind, zeal, passion, and stamina. Today, the spirit of Delilah strikes the minds of believers and targets their desire for God, lulling them to sleep so that the enemy can raid what they have been given. It releases an onslaught of constant pressure through words, threats, and manipulation. It seduces the army of God to a place of false comfort and safety, causing believers to romance the idea of Delilah until they are convinced that her knee is a place of refuge and rest. In reality, though, it is the epicenter of destruction.

You hold in your hands the blueprint of how this demonic spirit of destruction operates and how it lines up attacks against you with the intent to bring you down. In these pages, you will discover how to recognize an assault by the Delilah spirit based on the spiritual symptoms it causes. You will learn how to stop it from stealing your destiny as you take hold of the keys that will bring you into total victory.

1
WHAT IS THE SPIRIT OF DELILAH AND WHY IS IT AFTER YOU?

While I was attending a very well-known and popular conference, assembled with the objective to help pastors grow their churches and reach their community, I sat listening intently to the speakers, hoping to glean from experienced church builders useful principles I could implement to expand our church's vision and more effectively further God's kingdom. I was all in and ready to receive. I had my notebook in hand, feverishly taking notes. I was able to retain a lot of great information and content, but then it happened: I heard something I did not expect. One of the keynote speakers said something along these lines: "Pastors, you do not want to display the gifts of the Spirit up front from the stage or allow them to be highly visible in the altars. Guests and visitors might not understand what is happening and decide not to come back to your church. We advise that you have one service a month where you allow the gifts to flow freely. Advertise it as such so that everyone will know what to expect beforehand. They can choose to attend or not. This new method will broaden your appeal to the community."

As I heard that statement and witnessed how the church leaders in the audience so readily received it, I suddenly felt nauseous. I don't want to overembellish here, but I had a literal physical reaction to what I had heard. As I went to bed that night, I replayed the day's events in my mind. "Am I stuck in an old wineskin?" I asked myself. "Is this the new way that God is building His church? Am I trapped in a spirit of religion, like the Pharisees were? Could it be that Jesus does desire His church to be comfortable to those in sin instead of being a place of conviction?"

In my last book, *The Triple Threat Anointing*, I wrote about an encounter I had with Jesus in a dream. He showed me a coming movement of mass salvation, healing, and deliverance. The new cutting-edge methods taught at this conference were in opposition to what Jesus had revealed to me.

Just as I was thinking this, I heard the voice of the Holy Spirit ask me a question: "Will you close the door to Me too?"

I fell to my knees, weeping. "No, I want You!" I replied urgently. "Please come and don't leave me. I don't care if I never have a megachurch or if everyone gets offended. I want You to be front and center. I don't want You ever offended! I won't hide Your gifts, nor will I exile Your power to a back room out of a desire for man's acceptance."

At that moment, it was as if God pulled back the veil and exposed the spirit that has invaded the church and is actively at work to destroy the faith of believers. It is not a new spirit but one that has been around for a long time. In recent years, it has expanded its reach and gained disturbing momentum. God revealed to me the name of the spirit behind the movement that church planters have widely embraced, which has opened the door for many Christians to fall prey to its destructive power. The Lord said to me, "It is the spirit of Delilah."

THE BIRTH OF GOD'S CHAMPION

After God unveiled the Delilah spirit to me, He told me that He wanted to reveal more about this spirit to the church. I knew the basics of the story of Samson and Delilah. I had preached many sermons on the text, which is found in the book of Judges. Nonetheless, I knew that the Holy Spirit wanted to uncover a more profound truth than the infamous haircut that brought defeat to Israel's great judge and deliverer.

Samson was born when the nation of Israel had come under servitude to the Philistines because of its sin. Like many other biblical characters, Samson was born to a woman who was barren. Manoah, Samson's father, was from the tribe of Dan and lived in the city of Zorah. Manoah and his wife, who is unnamed in the Bible, were unable to have children. One day, an angel of the Lord appeared to the barren woman and told her that she would conceive and give birth to a son. Moreover, he said her son would be a Nazirite from his birth until his death and that he would begin to deliver Israel out of the hand of their oppressors.

> For behold, you shall conceive and give birth to a son. No razor shall come upon his head, for the boy shall be a Nazirite [dedicated] to God from birth; and he shall begin to rescue Israel from the hands of the Philistines.   (Judges 13:5 AMP)

Amazingly, even though God had allowed the Israelites to be given over into servitude because of their sin, He had already planned their deliverance. God always makes a way of escape for His children.

Manoah's wife excitedly ran and told her husband of the visit of the heavenly messenger and his announcement. Manoah immediately asked God to allow His angel to return to them for further instruction. The Lord granted Manoah's request, and the angel returned.

> *So Manoah asked him, "When your words come true, what kind of rules should govern the boy's life and work?" The angel of the LORD replied, "Be sure your wife follows the instructions I gave her. She must not eat grapes or raisins, drink wine or any other alcoholic drink, or eat any forbidden food."...Then Manoah took a young goat and a grain offering and offered it on a rock as a sacrifice to the LORD. And as Manoah and his wife watched, the LORD did an amazing thing. As the flames from the altar shot up toward the sky, the angel of the LORD ascended in the fire. When Manoah and his wife saw this, they fell with their faces to the ground.*
>
> (Judges 13:12–14, 19–20 NLT)

Moreover, verse 22 reveals that God's angel was, in fact, none other than Jesus Christ: *"And he said to his wife, 'We will certainly die, for we have seen God!'"* (Judges 13:22 NLT). What a birth announcement! Can you imagine what it must have been like for them to have received such news, having been childless for years? Suddenly, their world was transformed by a visit from God, who proclaimed to them that they would have a son. Not only would they have a baby, but God would use their son to shift the trajectory of their nation. This is the purpose of the church. This is God's purpose for you! You, as a part of the church, are called to legislate on earth the will of heaven. Christians are God's entryways on the earth.

At this point, let's pause and consider a common question: Is it scriptural to pray for God to allow you to have angelic visitations? Manoah's example bears witness to it. With that said, you must be careful not to exalt angelic activity or any supernatural demonstration over God Himself. There have been times when I have seen individuals and even churches get out of balance by glorifying supernatural encounters. Remember, the enemy can give you supernatural experiences, too. That is why you must use discernment and remain resolute in your pursuit of God.

The narrative goes on to inform us that Manoah's wife indeed bore a son and named him Samson. *"And the child grew, and the* LORD *blessed him. And the Spirit of the* LORD *began to move him at times in the camp of Dan between Zorah and Eshtaol"* (Judges 13:24–25).

The words *"to move"* were translated from the Hebrew word *pa'am,* defined by *Strong's Concordance* as "to tap, to beat regularly, to impel, to agitate," and "to trouble." As Samson began to grow, the Holy Spirit began to impel or trouble him to act. This verse reminds me of David when he heard Goliath mocking the God of Israel and was moved to stand against the giant. He asked the question, *"Is there not a cause?"* (1 Samuel 17:29). Whenever you are driven by the Spirit, no matter how impossible things may look in the natural, you will be empowered by the Holy Spirit to accomplish the feat.

When the power of God to bring miraculous results came on Samson, he was able to do in the natural that which was not possible for any ordinary man to do. The anointing is supernatural. It adds super to your natural. The anointing on Samson's life enabled him to gain many victories over the Philistines.

A DESCENT INTO COMPROMISE

Sometimes, when an individual is powerfully anointed of God, they will begin to take it for granted and even expect that the anointing will always flow through them no matter what they do or how they live. I have seen men and women who have been greatly anointed of God become lax in their relationship with the Lord. Rather than guard and protect their anointing, they started to abuse it. This was the case with Samson. Although he was a Nazirite from birth, chosen and anointed by God, he allowed himself to slowly descend into compromise.

A note of warning here: if you, as a believer, are not diligent to hear and obey the voice of the Holy Spirit, allowing Him to deal with your heart, you, too, can become vulnerable like Samson and plunge into a spiral of compromise. Through the life of Samson, a vivid picture is painted of the consequences of focusing only on your outward victories without allowing the Holy Spirit to deal with your internal struggles. The same Spirit that anoints you for service is the same Spirit who wants to free you from the weight of bondage that you carry in secret.

AN UNLAWFUL WIFE

In Judges 14:1–2 we can find a lot of insight into Samson's internal struggle—particularly how he begins to compromise with fleshly desires.

> *And Samson went down to Timnath, and saw a woman in Timnath of the daughters of the Philistines. And he came up, and told his father and his mother, and said, I have seen a woman in Timnath of the daughters of the Philistines: now therefore get her for me to wife.* (Judges 14:1–2)

Notice that the above verses stress that he "*saw a woman.*" The warning for all believers here is to guard their vision and be careful where they allow their eyes to focus. I cannot emphasize enough that Samson's decline began with his eyes. The enemy was after Samson's vision from the very beginning. He knew that Samson was anointed of God to be a deliverer of God's people.

Vision is a powerful thing in the life of any individual. Psalm 29:18 tells us, "*Where there is no vision, the people perish.*" When an individual's vision has been stolen, the person will cast off all restraint.

Take note that the enemy gained entry into Samson's life by fiercely attacking his eyes, meaning Satan's assault came through the realm of Samson's sight. Satan's ultimate goal was to make God's chosen vessel an embarrassment and a reproach upon Israel. He used the strategy to tempt Samson with lust for the very things from which God had called him to deliver Israel—the Philistines. The Philistine nation oppressed Israel, but his sexual desire for their women oppressed Samson.

Samson's parents tried to dissuade him from marrying a woman who did not share their faith. They recognized that a Philistine wife could mean trouble for Samson. It was unlawful for an Israelite to marry a woman who was of the lineage of the Philistines, (See Deuteronomy 7:3.) It was entirely reckless for Samson, as a Nazirite who had vowed to be separate and utterly devoted to the Lord, to make a covenant by becoming one with a worshipper of the false god Dagon. *"Is there no woman among the daughters of your relatives, or among all our people, that you must go to take a wife from the uncircumcised (pagan) Philistines?"* (Judges 14:3 AMP), his parents asked. Here is Samson's response: *"Get her for me, because she looks pleasing to me"* (Judges 14:3 AMP).

The writer of Judges goes on to note, *"His father and mother didn't realize the LORD was at work in this, creating an opportunity to work against the Philistines, who ruled over Israel at that time"* (Judges 14:4 NLT). Here we have a clear example of how God can take believers' foolish decisions and turn them for good. The Lord used Samson's dastardly mistake as an occasion to strike out against Israel's enemy. We see an acceleration of the Spirit moving upon Samson to accomplish incredible feats during this time.

Then Samson went down to Timnah with his father and mother [to arrange the marriage], and they came as far as the vineyards of Timnah; and suddenly, a young lion came roaring toward him. The Spirit of the LORD came upon him mightily, and he tore the lion apart as one tears apart a young goat, and he had nothing at all in his hand; but he did not tell his father or mother what he had done.

(Judges 14:5–6 AMP)

My kids and I watched a cartoon about Samson the other night. The animation depicted him as a vast, muscular, Hercules-type figure. However, this picture could not have been accurate, because the Philistines were desperate to know the secret to his strength. His great might was not due to his muscular physique. It was directly correlated with the Holy Spirit moving upon him. It was not through natural means but rather came through supernatural means; his might came through almighty God.

A BROKEN VOW

Samson tended always to take things one step too far. The Spirit of the Lord anointed him to kill the roaring lion with his bare hands, but later, once again, his eyes enticed him to break his vow to God.

When he returned later…he turned aside to see the carcass of the lion; and behold, a swarm of bees and honey were in the body of the lion. So he scraped the honey out into his hands and went on, eating as he went. When he came to his father and mother, he gave them some, and they ate it; but he did not tell them he had taken the honey from the body of the lion.

(Judges 14:8–9 AMP)

Samson's Nazirite vow strictly forbade him to touch dead things, but that did not stop Samson. He saw the swarm of bees in the lion's carcass and scraped the honey out of it.

The Spirit of the Lord always came upon him even after he had made poor choices. "Surely, it won't hurt to give me a forbidden treat this once," he may have thought. This is how Satan works against an individual and against the church at large. If one compromises first on one thing and then lowers their standards on another, the enemy will soon overtake that person.

Next, the story tells us that Samson, at his wedding to the Philistine woman, thought to entertain his guests with a riddle he had made up and alone knew the answer to. He even put forth a wager that no one would be able to solve the riddle. He was right: no one could come up with the answer. Here is where the story gets interesting. Samson's new Philistine bride was threatened by some wedding guests who told her to do whatever was necessary to gain the answer from Samson, or else they would burn down her father's house, along with every member of his household. She wept before Samson for the seven-day wedding festival and continually pressed him for the answer.

> So Samson's wife wept before him and said, "You only hate me, you do not love me; you have asked my countrymen a riddle, and have not told [the answer] to me." And he said to her, "Listen, I have not told my father or my mother [either], so [why] should I tell you?" However Samson's wife wept before him seven days while their [wedding] feast lasted, and on the seventh day he told her because she pressed him so hard.
>
> (Judges 14:16–17 AMP)

The behaviors Samson's wife exhibits here are all traits found in the spirit of Delilah. It will do whatever is necessary to get what it wants. Samson finally relented and revealed the answer to the riddle to his new bride, and she quickly relayed the answer to the Philistine men who had made the wager with Samson. His love for this Philistine woman, followed by her betrayal, was the precursor to the events that would lead to his ultimate failure.

A SERIES OF VENGEFUL MURDERS

Samson became so angry, and no doubt hurt, as well, at his wife's treachery that he left the wedding. Then the Spirit of the

Lord came upon him, and he killed thirty Philistine men. He took the spoils of the dead Philistines and gave them as payment to the men who had learned from his wife the answer to the riddle. Samson then went back to his father's house.

After some time had elapsed, Samson calmed down and decided to go and visit his wife, who had betrayed him; when he arrived, to his dismay, he discovered that her father had given her away to another man. Watch what he did next:

> *Samson said to them, "This time I shall be blameless in regard to the Philistines when I do them harm." So Samson went and caught three hundred foxes, and took torches and turning the foxes tail to tail, he put a torch between each pair of tails. When he had set the torches ablaze, he let the foxes go into the standing grain of the Philistines, and he burned up the heap of sheaves and the standing grain, along with the vineyards and olive groves.* (Judges 15:3–5 AMP)

The Philistines were furious and demanded to know who was responsible for burning their fields. When they discovered it was Samson, they burned Samson's wife and her father's household in retaliation. Then Philistines surrounded the men of Judah and announced that they had come to bind Samson. The men of Judah were terrified. They questioned why Samson had stirred up the anger of the Philistines who ruled over them. They could not comprehend why he would make it worse for them, his own people. Three thousand men of Judah confronted Samson. He agreed to be bound and turned over to the Philistines, but with the condition that none of his own people would bring any harm to him. They took Samson, bound him, and delivered him to their enemy. The Philistines began to shout against him. Suddenly, the Spirit of the Lord once again came upon Samson, and he broke the cords that bound him. He then found the jawbone of a donkey and killed one thousand men with it!

Samson had experienced a great victory, but he had again broken his Nazirite vow by touching the carcass of an animal. Next we see a vivid illustration of a profound truth: whenever there is a compromise, depletion follows. This time his compromise left him thirsty to the point of death, forcing Samson to cry out to God for mercy and provision.

> *Samson was very thirsty, and he called out to the LORD and said, "You have given this great victory through the hand of Your servant, and now am I to die of thirst and fall into the hands of the uncircumcised (pagans)?"* (Judges 15:18 AMP)

The Spirit of the Lord still assisted him, despite his having broken his vow. God, who is rich in mercy, heard and answered him.

> *God split open the hollow place that was at Lehi, and water came out of it. When Samson drank, his spirit (strength) returned, and he was revived. Therefore, he named it En-hakkore (spring which is calling), which is at Lehi to this day.* (Judges 15:19 AMP)

Samson renamed the place in Lehi *"En-hakkore,"* meaning *"the caller's fountain,"* for God had provided Samson a fountain of water, which consequently came forth from the same jawbone of the donkey that he had used as a weapon to kill the Philistines! Remember this when you think God is finished with the source that He has used in the past to help you and to demonstrate His glory!

GOD IS FAITHFUL DESPITE OUR FLAWS

Did you know that God's ear is open to your cry, just as it was to Samson's? Scripture is replete with assurances that God answers when His people call on Him for help:

+ *"Call unto me, and I will answer thee"* (Jeremiah 33:3).

+ *"Thou art the* LORD *the God, who...didst see the affliction of our fathers in Egypt, and heardest their cry by the Red sea; and shewedst signs and wonders upon Pharaoh, and on all his servants, and on all the people of his land: for thou knewest that they dealt proudly against them. So didst thou get thee a name, as it is this day. And thou didst divide the sea before them, so that they went through the midst of the sea on the dry land; and their persecutors thou threwest into the deeps, as a stone into the mighty waters"* (Nehemiah 9:7, 9–11).

+ *"But when [Peter] saw the wind boisterous, he was afraid; and beginning to sink, he cried, saying, Lord, save me. And immediately Jesus stretched forth his hand, and caught him, and said unto him, O thou of little faith, wherefore didst thou doubt?"* (Matthew 14:30–31).

Notice that Samson was *"revived"* when he drank from God's fountain. When there is a cry, revival begins. You who are intercessors crying out to God to send rivers of living water, be encouraged. Revival is coming because God has heard your cries. He will show His mercy in miraculous ways.

THE LIES BEFORE THE FALL

There were other instances of Samson's, besides the touching of the jawbone of the donkey, when he was lax with the anointing of God upon his life. God did not make these transgressions public before the nation. God, in His great mercy, will always deal with His children privately before exposing them publicly. However, the best-known example of Samson's failure—which was made public—was his love for Delilah. She would be the catalyst to bring about his fall.

And it came to pass afterward, that he loved a woman in the valley of Sorek, whose name was Delilah. And the lords of the

Philistines came up unto her, and said unto her, Entice him,
and see wherein his great strength lieth, and by what means
we may prevail against him, that we may bind him to afflict
him; and we will give thee every one of us eleven hundred
pieces of silver. (Judges 16:4–5)

The word *"entice"* is translated from the Hebrew word *pathah*, defined as "to open, (in a sinister way) to delude, allure, deceive, enlarge, entice, flatter," and "persuade."

Although Delilah was indeed a real-life woman, a demonic spirit operated through her to destroy Samson. The demonic spirit of Delilah is still in operation today. It has gripped its claws around the throat of many believers in the church, and its agenda has not changed from Samson's day. The goal of the Delilah spirit is to entice you away from your kingdom authority and rob you of your strength. How does it do this? It starts with deception. Its ruse is to trick you into believing its lies, starting with your vision.

And Delilah said to Samson, Tell me, I pray thee, wherein thy
great strength lieth, and wherewith thou mightest be bound to
afflict thee. (Judges 16:6)

In the beginning, Samson did not reveal the truth to Delilah when she asked for the secret of his great strength. First, he told her that he would lose his strength if he were bound by seven bowstrings that had never been dried. She tied him up with bowstrings and then screamed, "The Philistines are here to capture you!" (See Judges 16:7–9.) Upon hearing her cry, Samson jumped up and with great ease broke the bowstrings off himself. She realized then that he had not told her the truth.

Again, she asked for his secret, and for the second time he did not tell her the truth. He said to her that if new ropes bound him, he would be as weak as the average man. So she tested his answer, but the new ropes proved not to be the kryptonite to his power.

She was relentless. For a third time, she pleaded with him for the answer to his great strength. *"Samson replied, 'If you were to weave the seven braids of my hair into the fabric on your loom and tighten it with the loom shuttle, I would become as weak as anyone else"* (Judges 16:13 NLT). Observe how Samson's resolve to protect his secret and guard his vow to God began to break down. His third answer, although false, was very close to the actual truth. He mentioned his hair, which alluded to the Nazirite vow that spoke of separation unto God.

Take note that you, the reader, benefit from knowing the outcome and recognizing how Delilah was setting Samson up. You might wonder how he could have been so blind. I would challenge you with this question: How many times have you been blinded to the enemy's attacks when others looking on could see what was happening to you?

We saw a glimpse of the Delilah spirit in the book of Genesis. Potiphar's wife did to Joseph the same exact thing that Delilah is doing to Samson here, for it was the identical spirit in operation. (See Genesis 39.) This same Delilah spirit works the same way in both stories, but the outcomes are different. In Genesis, Potiphar's wife did everything she could to seduce Joseph. However, Joseph did not fall into her trap. He would not entertain that spirit; instead, he removed himself from its presence. That's key: whenever a believer is under an attack from the Delilah spirit, they must not endure its words and continual pressure. If they do, they will eventually surrender to it just to get some relief. That's the outcome we find in the story of Samson. Scripture tells us that Delilah

> *pressed him daily with her words, and urged him, so that his*
> *soul was vexed unto death; that he told her all his heart, and*
> *said unto her, There hath not come to a razor upon mine head;*
> *for I have been a Nazarite unto God from my mother's womb:*
> *if I be shaven, then my strength will go from me, and I shall*
> *become weak, and be like any other man. And when Delilah*

saw that he had told her all his heart, she sent and called for the lords of the Philistines, saying, Come up this once, for he hath shewed me all his heart. (Judges 16:16–18)

Pay attention to what happened next:

She made him sleep upon her knees; and she called for a man, and she caused him to shave off the seven locks of his head; and she began to afflict him, and his strength went from him. And she said, The Philistines be upon thee, Samson. And he awoke out of his sleep, and said, I will go out as at other times before, and shake myself. And he wist not that the LORD was departed from him. (Judges 16:19–20)

While I was reading verse 19, the Holy Spirit spoke to me about breaking the stronghold of the spirit of Delilah. The Scripture says, "*She made him sleep upon her knees.*" If Samson had only awakened and realized what her influence and relationship would cost him, he would have fortified himself against her allure.

READY FOR A WAKE-UP CALL

Not long after the conference I attended and the message from the Lord that followed it, I was praying in my prayer room and was taken into a vision. I saw a battlefield and warriors loaded with weaponry, prepared for battle. As I looked, it seemed that, out of nowhere, their enemy came flying overhead and started dropping upon them what appeared to be thick, heavy drapes. To me, it seemed as if their foe was attempting to blanket them in heavy darkness. I heard the Lord's voice loudly roar, "No! It is broken! They are mantled with My authority!" As soon as He spoke, the enemy's blanket fell off God's warriors and disappeared.

After this vision, the Lord revealed more to me regarding the spirit of Delilah, taking me to the life of Samson, the great judge of Israel. I was already very familiar with the story of Samson, having preached many messages on his life, failure, and comeback. Yet the Lord said to me, "There is more in Samson's life for you to learn, and you must reveal it to My church for this hour." Moreover, He said,

> The Spirit of Delilah has lullabied My church to sleep. This Spirit seduces My chosen ones until they lay their head on its lap and sleep until it's too late. The enemy has overtaken them! Remember, at first, Samson was able to resist Delilah's maximum pressure tactics. His resolve was broken down little by little, and he ultimately gave way to her treacherous scheme. Sound the alarm! Expose its devious plots and dismantle its evil works! Awaken My warriors! It is not a time for them to submit to the spirit of Delilah. It is not the time to sleep while the adversary lays a snare for them. For no longer will My people be able to shake off their sin and still have the anointing operating through them. No more compromise! Say to My people, "Soldiers, take your positions, stand your ground, and fight! Get off Delilah's playground. It is time to war and win on the battleground. Get your head out of her lap and protect your anointing. Watchmen, arise, put on your armor, and use your weapons against the forces of hell. Now is your moment. Shake off the spirit of Delilah that has bewitched you. This is your set time.

The spirit of Delilah has lullabied the church to sleep. The enemy is crouching at the door, and the army of God has been put to sleep by the spirit of Delilah. The church must lift her head out of Delilah's lap.

The Spirit of God is calling to you, saying, "Wake up! You are being attacked. Don't become a casualty. Don't fall into the clutches of the Delilah spirit. Refuse to be lulled to sleep until there is no strength left in you. Get away from the spirit of Delilah. Instead, walk in your God-given victory and fulfill your assignment."

Refuse to allow Delilah to administer her anesthetic to you. Prepare for battle! The time has come for you to awaken from slumber. Revival, restoration, and renewal are here for you. You must stop the spirit of Delilah's reign of lethargic complacency.

For if the trumpet give an uncertain sound, who shall prepare himself to the battle? (1 Corinthians 14:8)

The message I have for you now is this: You are God's champion! Samson no longer lives on this earth, but you do! You are the one to whom God is referring in this book, the one He is warning to beware of the spirit of Delilah. Do you not realize that Satan is more terrified of you than you are of him? He fears you will receive and live by the life-changing revelation that you are called for *more!* He doesn't want you to gain knowledge of the spirit that is even now working to steal your joy, confuse your mind, and lull you to sleep. Cut off all ties with the spirit of Delilah. Wake up and stop it in its tracks!

PLAYTIME IS OVER

On another day while I was praying, the Lord showed me a different vision. In it I saw warriors that were equipped with the finest of military ware. They were armed with guns, ammunition, and all the weaponry of war. The enemy began dropping bombs and fighting heavily against them. Much to my shock, there was a child's merry-go-round in the middle of the battlefield. The warriors under siege left their positions and started to play on the merry-go-round. They were spinning round and round as if they hadn't a care in the world. Then the Lord said to me, "Tell My people that playtime is over!" God has supplied His children with everything they need to win in the battle against their adversary. However, the devil will send a plethora of distractions to keep them occupied and going round and round in the same cycles. It is time for God's army to arise from its comatose state. Believer, you have the power to put the enemy on the run from your life, your family, and your generation!

2

SPIRITUAL SYMPTOMS OF AN ATTACK BY DELILAH

When the Lord first gave to me the revelation concerning this ancient spirit, my response was to ask, "Why would the spirit of Delilah come after me? After all, I'm not Samson, killing Philistines left and right." The Lord quickly responded, "No, you are not Samson, but you are My champion. Just as Samson, Moses, David, and other saints of old, you too have a destiny. You have been called to advance My kingdom for My purpose, and Satan hates that I chose you."

CALLED TO A SPECIFIC PURPOSE

Do you know that you are called of God? You have a destiny that has been outlined and set into motion by the Creator of heaven and earth. The same God who put the stars in the sky, filled the seas with water, and created everything by the power of His Word formed you in your mother's womb for a purpose—or, more to the point, for *His purpose*.

Take Jeremiah, for example. He was created for God's purpose to be a prophet:

> *Before I formed thee in the belly I knew thee; and before thou camest forth out of the womb I sanctified thee, and I ordained thee a prophet unto the nations.*　　　　　(Jeremiah 1:5)

You are no less than Jeremiah. You too were created for God's purpose:

> *We know that all things work together for good to them that love God, to them who are the called according to **his purpose**. For whom he did foreknow, he also did predestinate to be conformed to the image of his Son, that he might be the firstborn among many brethren. Moreover whom he did predestinate, them he also called: and whom he called, them he also justified: and whom he justified, them he also glorified.*
> 　　　　　(Romans 8:28–30)

Did you see that? You are called according to His purpose! (See verse 28.) You were born to advance the Lord's plan on earth. The word *"predestinate,"* as used in verse 29, is the Greek word *proorízō*, meaning "to predetermine, to decide beforehand, to foreordain." That is mind-blowing to me. Think about it: God Himself chose you and me to be a part of His plan.

> *For this purpose the Son of God was manifested, that he might destroy the works of the devil.*　　　　　(1 John 3:8)

You might think that the enemy is not after you because you are not a minister or a preacher. Perhaps you are a businessperson, a stay-at-home parent, or a retail worker. Regardless of your profession, as a blood-bought child of God, you are His representative on the earth.

Then Jesus said to them again, "Peace to you; as the Father has sent Me, I also send you [as My representatives]."

(John 20:21 AMP)

You are here in an official capacity to represent Jesus and do His works in this generation. You are born for such a time as this, by God's design. Jesus came to destroy the works of the devil and now has commissioned you to do His works and even greater works.

I tell you the truth, anyone who believes in me will do the same works I have done, and even greater works, because I am going to be with the Father.   (John 14:12 NLT)

The enemy yearns to impede God's plan. Jesus has handed you the assignment of the works that He did, and even greater works. Are you ready for your supernatural mission?

Know this: Satan craves to devastate your destiny. He is a liar, thief, and a destroyer (see John 10:10). God created you for His purpose. Yes, you have a divine destiny. You are not called to live an average or carnal Christian life. No! You are God's ambassador on the earth. An *ambassador* is "a diplomatic official of the highest rank, sent by one sovereign or state to another as its resident representative."[1] Generally speaking, an ambassador is sent to a foreign kingdom or nation to reflect the official position of the sovereign that bestowed their authority upon them. When the apostle Paul wrote his letter to the church at Corinth, he used the description *"Christ's ambassadors"* (2 Corinthians 5:20 NIV) to refer to all believers. God has sent you to represent His kingdom upon the earth, and that is why the devil is keen on unleashing all his agents of darkness to war against you.

---

1. Dictionary.com, s.v. "ambassador," https://www.dictionary.com/browse/ambassador.

SYMPTOMS OF AN ATTACK OF DELILAH

Now we know why we're under attack. But do we know what it feels like to be under attack? In the remainder of this chapter and the next, we'll discuss some of the symptoms that indicate the spirit of Delilah has targeted us.

LOSS OF DESIRE FOR THE THINGS OF GOD

Lack of spiritual passion and zeal for the things of God is undoubtedly the number one identifier that Delilah has made headway in your life. Satan does not randomly throw out attacks against you just to see if they will stick. He and his demonic agents from hell have methodically and craftily studied your life. Satan looks for an entry point to carry out his sinister agenda. Satan masterfully orchestrates a steady rhythm of crises and distractions to invade your life.

During such attacks, you are surrounded on every side with circumstances vying for your attention. You begin to consider excuses like, "I am so busy, it won't hurt to skip my prayer time today," or "I'll read my Bible tomorrow." When this occurs, you can be assured that you have started along the journey toward losing your passion for the things of God.

Unresolved hurt and offense between you and others—even God—can result in Delilah stealing your longing for the presence of God and quenching your spiritual fire from blazing. Offense often occurs when things do not work out the way you hoped they would.

FEELING OFFENDED

Offense is a sly emotion that can quickly develop into a stronghold if left unconfronted, and it can happen even to the strongest of believers. Take, for example, John the Baptist. Jesus described him in glowing terms, saying, "*I tell you the truth, of all who have ever lived, none is greater than John the Baptist"* (Matthew 11:11 NLT). That was quite a statement for the Son of God to make about a man! Yet John, the one who was sent to prepare the way of the Lord and to preach the message that the kingdom of God is at hand, faced the temptation to be offended by his circumstances.

> *John the Baptist, who was in prison, heard about all the things the Messiah was doing. So he sent his disciples to ask Jesus, "Are you the Messiah we've been expecting, or should we keep looking for someone else?" Jesus told them, "Go back to John and tell him what you have heard and seen—the blind see, the lame walk, those with leprosy are cured, the deaf hear, the dead are raised to life, and the Good News is being preached to the poor." And he added, "God blesses those who do not fall away because of me."* (Matthew 11:2–6 NLT)

John was Jesus's cousin. He was a miracle baby. His parents were old when he was born, and his mother had been barren until God opened her womb. The Bible described John as being filled with the Holy Ghost in his mother's belly. (See Luke 1:15.) Like Samson, John was a Nazirite from birth. He was one of the first prophets to recognize and announce that Jesus was the Messiah.

> *The next day John seeth Jesus coming unto him, and saith, Behold the Lamb of God, which taketh away the sin of the world. This is he of whom I said, After me cometh a man which is preferred before me: for he was before me.* (John 1:29–30)

John baptized Jesus. He saw the heavens open. He witnessed the Holy Spirit descend upon Jesus like a dove. He heard the Father's booming voice proclaiming Jesus as the Son of God.

> *And Jesus, when he was baptized, went up straightway out of the water: and, lo, the heavens were opened unto him, and he saw the Spirit of God descending like a dove, and lighting*

upon him: and lo a voice from heaven, saying, This is my
beloved Son, in whom I am well pleased.

(Matthew 3:16–17)

When dire circumstances press in, even those who are considered to possess the strongest of faith—as in the case of John—can be tested beyond their normal endurance. John's imprisonment had weaved feelings of doubt and offense that made him question whether Jesus was indeed the promised Messiah. Notice that John experienced these misgivings while he was in prison. He was isolated, under heavy opposition, pressed on every side; this is the kind of steady rhythm of crises and distractions that I referred to earlier. John was a target of this kind of attack, and we are equally vulnerable to the temptations of doubt and offense.

Jesus told John's disciples to remind John that the prophetic word of God that had been foretold by the prophets was indeed being fulfilled: "The blind see again, the crippled walk, lepers are cured, the deaf hear, the dead are raised back to life, and the poor and broken now hear of the hope of salvation!" (See Luke 7:22.)

When you are under siege by the enemy, it is crucial that you cling to the Word. Read it! Speak it! Pray it! Listen to it! The Bible is the sword that cuts the head off the giant. The Word of God was the weapon that Jesus used against Satan in the desert when He was under attack. (See, for example, Luke 4:1–13.)

"It is written." That's how Jesus answered the devil when He was being tempted. (See, for example, Luke 4:4, 8, 10.) This phrase has become one of my favorites to declare. Whenever the enemy starts to combat your mind with doubts, accusations, and fear, make a declaration that begins, "It is written…" and follow it up with one of God's promises that contradict the lie that the devil is peddling.

WANING DESIRE FOR THE THINGS OF GOD

The enemy knows that if he is able steal or even dull your desire for the things of God and His presence, it will leave you vulnerable to him so that he can fill that void with a variety of other things. Anything that moves you away from God is from the enemy. Evaluate your relationships, activities, hobbies, and entertainment sources to see whether they drive you away from God or draw you toward Him.

One day I had the television on in the background while I was doing some work on my computer. The television show was *Divorce Court*. I heard the Holy Spirit ask me, "Why are you being entertained by something that I hate? You are allowing strife and fighting into your home through your television." I quickly repented and took authority over any spirit that I had invited into my home. Some people may call me legalistic or accuse me of going overboard. I say take it up with the Holy Spirit. I would rather be too radical in what I avoid than find out later that I should never have allowed it.

DEPARTURE FROM YOUR "FIRST WORKS"

Samson had traded his intimacy with God for intimacy with Philistine women. The enemy wants you to desire forbidden things that will decrease your hunger for God. It is critical that you continue to stoke the fire of personal revival in your life. I know ministers who constantly preach on revival and pray for revival for their church services, but their own lifestyles are not those of someone who is living revived.

Revival is not a series of meetings or a gimmick to draw people to church. Revival is birthed in the prayer room, not on a platform. Corporate revival is the overflow of personal revival. For you to blaze with the fire of God, you must be intentional. What I mean is that you must purposefully carve out a path for God to ignite you. The apostle Paul instructed his spiritual son Timothy to "*fan into a flame and rekindle the fire of the spiritual gift God imparted to you"* (2 Timothy 1:6 TPT), meaning "excite the gift" or "awake the gift." In other words, he exhorted Timothy to stoke the fire of God within him and cause it to burn ever brighter.

How do you fan the flame or birth personal revival in your life? John the Revelator wrote to the church of Ephesus regarding the subject of revival, telling them how to experience it in their lives:

> *Thou hast left thy first love. Remember therefore from whence thou art fallen, and repent, and do the first works; or else I will come unto thee quickly, and will remove thy candlestick out of his place, except thou repent.*   (Revelation 2:5)

John's instructions were for the church to *"repent, and do the first works."* How does that apply to you as you read this book? If you have lost your hunger for the things of God, and His presence no longer moves you, you are in danger. There is a loud warning alarm that is sounding to you today. The spirit of Delilah is trying to buffet God's plan for your life. This spirit is trying to lull you to sleep. First, you must recognize that you are under assault. Second, you must repent of any areas where you have compromised. And, third, you must return to your first works.

What did John mean by *"return to your first works"*? Remember when you first fell in love with Jesus? One of my favorite things is to pastor brand-new believers. Most times, they are completely over the moon in love with Jesus. Everything about Him excites them. Just saying His name moves them. You must get excited about Jesus. To return to your first works means to go back to that which drew you to Him in the first place.

I met with a couple one day who were having problems in their marriage. As we began to talk, the wife started describing how the husband was glued to sports and had no interest in what she enjoyed doing. The husband began to complain that his wife never spent time with him or gave him the attention he desired.

I interrupted them both and asked, "What was it like when you were dating?" I wanted to find out what had changed. We discovered that what had changed were their first works—how they had acted at the beginning of their relationship. He would bring her flowers. She would laugh at his corny jokes. Sadly, they had grown distant because they had not intentionally kept up their first works.

When a couple has been married for a long time, it is easy to take that covenant for granted. If you are not careful, you can grow apart and soon be living totally separate lives. It is necessary for a married couple to nurture their relationship and do what they did at the beginning of their courtship. It is the same with our relationship with the Lord. Even though God's love is perfect, and He loves us unconditionally, it is our love for Him that we must continue to stoke.

You were made with a void that only time in the Lord's presence can fill. Whenever you allow anything besides Jesus to fill that void, you must repent and return to your first works.

SPIRITUAL FATIGUE AND BATTLE WEARINESS

Have you ever felt unusually tired for no apparent reason? I am not referring to natural tiredness, which we all experience from time to time and which can be quickly remedied by nurturing our bodies with adequate rest, nutritious food, and minimized stress. I'm speaking of a supernatural type of tiredness and fatigue.

I remember an episode in my life when I felt exhausted and could not get past my fatigue, no matter how much I slept or how deeply I rested. "I'm so tired!" I kept saying, over and over, to whoever was near me (usually my wife). There was no reason in the natural for my body to be feeling that way.

At one point when I told my wife (again) that I was tired, the words had scarcely left my lips when I heard the Holy Spirit say,

"This is an attack of the enemy. You are not physically tired. You are fighting fatigue and battle weariness."

I soon discovered that fatigue is one of the enemy's favorite tactics against believers. When the enemy targets you with fatigue and battle weariness, he plagues your mind with thoughts of deception to stop you from getting to the root of the problem. At the time, I had a barrage of thoughts distracting me from the things of God. I thought I could bounce back if I could just have another vacation. The truth was that I was under assault from the enemy. He had come to drain my strength and to weary me until I no longer saw the opposition I was facing from my adversary.

Fatigue is defined as "weariness from bodily or mental exertion; a slow ordeal."[2] Whenever the enemy launches an assault of fatigue, it causes you to grow weary in battle. Notice that fatigue is a "slow ordeal." It is a process of breaking you down little by little until weariness becomes your identity.

When God exposed the enemy's attack against me, He reminded me of this Scripture: "*Let us not **grow weary** or become discouraged in doing good*" (Galatians 6:9 AMP). The Holy Spirit inspired here an interesting choice of words. You need to get this point: for something to grow, it must be nourished. The Holy Spirit is telling you to *stop nourishing spiritual fatigue!*

The Lord revealed to me that the temptation to faint comes just before we step into a new season of reaping. I implore you to arise and take authority over the enemy of your soul when he comes to ravage you with fatigue, preventing you from growing in the things of God. Don't give a place to Satan's weariness.

BATTLE FATIGUE

The apostle Paul wrote to the church at Thessalonica to minister to those facing such an attack:

---

2. Dictionary.com, s.v. "fatigue," https://www.dictionary.com/browse/fatigue.

We appeal to you, dear brothers and sisters, to instruct those who are not in their place of battle. Be skilled at gently encouraging those who feel themselves inadequate. Be faithful to stand your ground. Help the weak stand again. Be quick to demonstrate patience with everyone.

(1 Thessalonians 5:14 TPT)

Take note that Paul encouraged the believers to minister to those who were not in their place of battle. Have you left your place of battle? Have you forfeited ground to the enemy because you feel tired? There have been times that I have fallen into this temptation. I unknowingly gave up territory to the enemy. The apostle Paul's phrase *"those who feel themselves inadequate"* can also be translated as "those who are losing heart or fainthearted."

Last year, I was taken into yet another vision of a battlefield full of warriors. These warriors were scattered all over, and as I watched, a thick fog covered the land so heavily that it clouded the soldiers' vision. I could perceive that they were struggling over what they were to do. Were they to go forward? Turn in another direction? They were in a state of internal and external confusion, and their perplexity caused them to grow weary. They began to sit down precisely where they had been standing, no longer taking ground or advancing. They were *stuck.* The Lord instructed me that this was a prophetic picture of what the enemy has done to many believers. He told me to prophesy that the fog is lifting, and clarity is coming. Stand up again, child of God. The captain of the Lord's army is on your side.

The enemy often uses battle fatigue to prompt believers to remove themselves from the place of battle altogether. They simply give up. In the *Amplified Version,* the apostle Paul describes such ones as *"those who are out of line"* (1 Thessalonians 5:14 AMP). The spirit of Delilah wants to move you out of your assignment and into its lap, where you are vulnerable for it to strike out against you.

STEPPING OUT OF YOUR PLACE IN BATTLE

Earlier in my pastoral ministry, we had a family visit our assembly. The husband had been debating whether to even go to church because he had been emotionally hurt and had fallen out of fellowship with God. I will never forget the week that the family first attended our church. The Holy Spirit saturated that service and moved mightily.

Later, I met with the husband at a local coffee shop. As soon as I joined him at his table, I was caught a little off guard because we had barely greeted one another when he started to sob. This man was robust and strong. He actively served in the military. He was not someone you would expect to see sobbing in a coffee shop.

He told me how greatly he had been impacted by the services his family had attended at our church. He described to me how he had previously served as an associate pastor at a church in another city. He explained how he had been hurt in the church, having been under constant pressure that caused him to become weary and fatigued. He had resigned from that position and moved his family across the country after giving away his entire study library, and he thought he wanted nothing more to do with ministry.

He went on to explain that when he had started coming to our church, the Holy Spirit began working on him. God had been speaking to him in his dreams, and a hunger for God suddenly returned to him. God began ministering healing and restoration to him. He said his wife was in awe of God as she watched his fire for the Lord reignite.

After several months of mentoring, Bible study, and prayer times together, I asked this man to join our leadership team. He gladly accepted and went on to help start several ministries within our church.

During this time, we had two influential families in our church begin to walk in rebellion as they planted and nurtured seeds of offense. They eventually left to start their own church. Those who have served as a pastor or have led a ministry know that this is sadly par for the core. The man naively felt that he needed to meet with the two families who were damaging the church. He thought they would see the error of their ways and repent if he could just talk to them. In an effort to protect him, I advised him that it was not wise to do so. My wife and I had already spoken with these couples, confronted the spirit of rebellion, and given them the opportunity to repent and be reconciled—only to have them insist on following through with their plan. I explained to him that while we needed to pray for them, it was senseless to try reasoning with them, as you cannot reason with someone under the sway of a demonic spirit. I knew their heart was in no condition to hear the truth and repent. They intended to cause maximum damage as they made their exit.

The next Sunday, this man was not at the pre-service prayer. I knew in my spirit that something was wrong, for he rarely missed it. He then came in late to the morning service and sat in the back with his arms crossed instead of freely worshipping in the altar. His demeanor had changed. I knew immediately that the spirit of deception had jumped over onto him. He had fallen prey to demonic manipulation.

I called him that afternoon and asked if he had met with the offended families. He verified that he had. A short time later, his church attendance began to wane, and he resigned from leading the groups that he had helped birth—all because he had stepped out of the place of battle. There is no doubt in my mind that God had called him to the church. Yet when he stepped out of alignment and refused to heed spiritual counsel, it opened the door to the enemy.

GET UP!

Satan can plan an attack against you and execute it, but he has no way of seeing into the future to know the outcome of the attack.

He only knows how effective it was by how *you* react to his strike. Only God is omniscient, having the attribute of being all-knowing. Satan cannot see into the future.

The day I discovered the ministry betrayal from the rebellious families, I was devastated. I went upstairs to my prayer room. While I was lying on the floor, curled up in a ball, the only words I could muster were, "God, I'm wounded. I am bleeding. This time it was too much, and I am really wounded." Right then, I heard God speak to me, "Shut up! Put on your armor and quit letting the devil know how wounded you feel. I am your healer. Open your mouth and prophesy your way out of this brokenness. Declare that I am your healer and watch me move for you."

Child of God, get up from the place of brokenness. Put on your armor. Stand strong and refuse to allow the enemy to weary you. You are on the verge of stepping into victory and possessing the spoils of the enemy.

TORMENTING THOUGHTS

One of the greatest weapons the enemy has in his arsenal to use against believers is to flood our minds with thoughts contrary to the Word of God. He delights when one of God's chosen vessels dwells on his tormenting thoughts.

Joyce Meyer wrote the landmark book *Battlefield of the Mind*. It is even more relevant today than it was when she wrote it. In her book, Joyce wrote, "Our actions are a direct result of our thoughts. If we have a negative mind, we will have a negative life. If, on the other hand, we renew our mind according to God's Word, we will, as Romans 12:2 promises, prove out in our experience 'the good and acceptable and perfect will of God' for our lives."[3]

---

3. Joyce Meyer, *Battlefield of the Mind* (New York: Warner Books, 1995), 12.

I would like to take the subject a step further and say: *Your victory or defeat* **begins** *with a thought.* Consider that declarative statement. Your victory hinges on your thought life.

You are probably familiar with the children's book *The Little Engine That Could.* It is the story of a little blue train engine that tried to climb a hill, and although it had never accomplished such a feat, it still tried. With every advance it made upward, it repeated what is now a familiar line today: "I think I can. I think I can." This folk story was meant to encourage the reader to think with optimism that they, like the little blue train engine, can accomplish whatever task lies ahead of them.

The truth found within that children's tale is profound. I ask you, what are your thoughts telling you? Are your thoughts lined up with the little blue train engine, with the "I think I can" attitude? Or are you making excuses for why you cannot accomplish your goal? Your victory or defeat are found in a thought. *"For as he thinketh in his heart, so is he"* (Proverbs 23:7).

FALLING PREY TO A THREEFOLD STRONGHOLD

When the Lord started to bring me out of a three-year battle with demonic depression, He exposed one of the main tactics the enemy had used to gain a stronghold in my life. Satan had planted negative thoughts in my mind that I had begun dwelling on instead of casting them down. In essence, I was putting my faith in those thoughts. I unknowingly came into agreement with Satan's lies. That is what we do every time we embrace a thought that goes against what God has decreed about us.

When I was a little boy, my mother preached a sermon on how the devil moves in threes. I am sure you have heard the saying "Trouble comes in threes." It is true. In her message, she focused on how the enemy progresses with "thoughts, imaginations, and strongholds." He begins with a thought. If we receive that thought and dwell on it, it moves us into an imagination. Suddenly, it is no longer a mere passing thought. It is an imagination. Then the enemy advances his agenda into the final stage by making a stronghold in the center of our life. A stronghold is a place of sure footing for the enemy. In other words, he has gained access into our life to bring about destruction, and it all began with a lying thought.

In his letter to the church at Corinth, the apostle Paul instructed believers to cast down everything that exalts itself against God and to bring every thought into "captivity" to the obedience of Christ. (See 2 Corinthians 10:5.) The principle here is that when a deceiving or corrupt thought crosses your mind, you have the authority to bring it into captivity. I love how this Scripture is translated in *The Passion Translation*:

> *We can demolish every deceptive fantasy that opposes God and break through every arrogant attitude that is raised up in defiance of the true knowledge of God. We capture, like prisoners of war, every thought and insist that it bow in obedience to the Anointed One.* (2 Corinthians 10:5 TPT)

A threefold cord is not easily broken (see Ecclesiastes 4:12), but it can be. With deceptive thoughts, imaginations, and strongholds, Satan thinks he has you—but he is a liar. You can still escape his strongholds. It is not easy to do—the Word is clear on that—but it can be done through the renewing of the mind!

TAKING THOUGHTS CAPTIVE

When God first revealed to me the power of my thoughts, I happened to be shopping at Walmart. I had recently been delivered from three years of depression and experienced the power of God in a new way. As I was pushing my grocery cart around the store, suddenly, a barrage of tormenting thoughts flooded my mind: "You're not good enough. No one loves you. You're an embarrassment to God." Satan was hurling his lying accusations at me. But then I heard the voice of my Father: "Andrew, I would never tell you anything that goes against what My Word says about you. It is the enemy. He is trying to make you believe his lies and lead you back into depression. Take authority over him NOW!"

Right there, still pushing my grocery cart, I began to rebuke the devil. Sometimes you must become very aggressive with the enemy. Other people probably thought I was crazy that day, walking through the store saying, "I bind you, devil. I am the head and not the tail. I am above and not beneath. I am the lender and not the borrower. I am highly favored of God and men. The blood of Jesus has redeemed me. I am a joint-heir with Christ." However, I had already reached a place of not caring what other people thought. I was in a fight and didn't have time to play. I had to take those thoughts captive.

> *The weapons of our warfare are not physical [weapons of flesh and blood]. Our weapons are divinely powerful for the destruction of fortresses. We are destroying sophisticated arguments and every exalted and proud thing that sets itself up against the [true] knowledge of God, and we are taking every thought and purpose captive to the obedience of Christ.*
> (2 Corinthians 10:4–5 AMP)

The spirit of Delilah delights in tormenting its prey. *The Message* Bible says it like this: "[Delilah] *kept at it day after day, nagging and tormenting* [Samson]. *Finally, he was fed up—he couldn't take another minute of it*" (Judges 16:16 MSG). Her constant pressure and cutting words left Samson wishing for death.

Maybe, as you are reading this, you have just come through an attack by the Delilah spirit. Maybe you are currently fighting its torments. You may be at the place where Samson was, or where I have been, where you just can't take another minute of it. Here is the good news: God has orchestrated this day to be your day of deliverance. Take authority over the tormenting thoughts. Cast down the vain imaginations. Pull down the strongholds the enemy has erected in your life. Jesus paid the price with His blood for you to be free from Satan's grip.

You may ask, "How do you stay free?" The secret to staying free is found in staying in the Bible. I vividly remember the moment God came and met with me as I sat in my living room. He instantaneously freed me. Yet He did not stop there. He taught me the way to keep my newfound freedom. I learned that I had to have a new mind—or, I should say, a *renewed* mind. Paul tells us in Romans 12:2, "*Be not conformed to this world: but be ye transformed by the renewing of your mind.*" I like the way the *New Living Translation* renders this entire verse:

> *Don't copy the behavior and customs of this world, but let God transform you into a new person by changing the way you think. Then you will learn to know God's will for you, which is good and pleasing and perfect.*　(Romans 12:2 NLT)

God transforms you into a new person by changing the way you think!

PURSUE YOUR PURPOSE

The spirit of Delilah is after you because you are called of God to fulfill a special purpose. Your ultimate adversary, Satan, who empowers the Delilah spirit, hates that God loves you.

Satan goes by many names, one of which is Lucifer. The name Lucifer means "morning star and light-bearer." He was initially entrusted with guarding the glory of God and bearing the light radiating from God. The prophet Ezekiel has this to say about him:

> *Thou sealest up the sum, full of wisdom, and perfect in beauty. Thou hast been in Eden the garden of God; every precious stone was thy covering, the sardius, topaz, and the diamond, the beryl, the onyx, and the jasper, the sapphire, the emerald,*

*and the carbuncle, and gold: the workmanship of thy tabrets
and of thy pipes was prepared in thee in the day that thou wast
created.* (Ezekiel 28:12–13)

Notice that Ezekiel uses superlatives like *"full of wisdom,"*
"perfect in beauty," and being *"the seal of perfection"* (Ezekiel 28:12
NIV) to describe him. This text shows that Lucifer was created
with the most beautiful attributes of all God's creation. In verse
13, the word translated *"workmanship"* comes from the Hebrew
word *m'lâ'kâh*, meaning "occupation, work," and "business." This
passage implies that Lucifer led worship before the throne of
God, even having instruments and pipes created in him. The word
"tabrets" is from the Hebrew word *tôph*, meaning "a tambourine,
tabret" and "timbrel."

Yet Lucifer became so captivated by his own wisdom, beauty,
position, and splendor that pride filled his heart: "Your heart was
filled with pride because of all your beauty. Your wisdom was corrupted by your love of splendor. So I threw you to the ground and
exposed you to the curious gaze of kings" (Ezekiel 28:17 NLT).
Lucifer desired for himself the glory and honor that belonged to
God.

Pride was the iniquity that caused Satan to be cast down
from heaven. I am sure he wonders why God would choose flawed
human beings to worship Him. "How could these sinful createures
have replaced me?" he must often ask himself.

Scripture warns us,

*The time is coming—indeed it's here now—when true wor-
shippers will worship the Father in spirit and in truth. The
Father is looking for those who will worship him that way.*
(John 4:23 NLT)

I must be clear: we are in a spiritual war, and the consequences
are eternal. Though this battle is invisible, it is very real. We are

constantly bombarded by agents of the evil one, including the spirit of Delilah.

Know this, child of God: Jesus came to give you an abundant life. It is time to arise and take authority over the tormenting lies of the devil. You belong to Jesus Christ! Now rule and reign as a royal child of the King. Break free from the chains the devil has sent to bind you. Develop the mentality of an overcomer!

3

COUNTERFEIT, COMPROMISE, AND THOUGHTS OF SUICIDE

Before I proposed to my wife, Brooke, I saved up money in anticipation of getting her the perfect ring that I knew that she would love. I had saved for months. I can still remember walking into the jewelry store with my mom and grandmother in tow; they had agreed to come as official style advisors. I carefully communicated every detail to the ring designer, who sketched out the design to my specifications. It was an amazing process of visually seeing your vision come to life. After several weeks of emails back and forth between the ring designer and me, the day finally arrived when I was to pick up the ring. I vividly remember walking into the jewelry store and finally seeing the ring. It looked precisely the way I had imagined it in my mind. I could not wait to give it to the woman I hoped would become my wife.

Brooke had always dreamed of getting engaged under the Christmas tree in New York City's Rockefeller Center. When she was a child, even her Barbies would get proposed to beneath a pretend Rockefeller Christmas tree. Knowing her dream, I orchestrated a trip to New York City, and I had worked everything out—or so I thought. I booked our flights. I used Hilton points to book separate hotel rooms for us. I had arranged for a car to pick us up at the airport and transport us to the hotel. I was on top of everything.

The one thing I had yet to decide was whether to pack the engagement ring in my checked luggage or my carry-on bag. The thought of airport security pulling out the ring and spoiling the surprise raced through my mind. I imagined having to propose at the TSA checkpoint. Wouldn't that be romantic? In the end, the thought of the ring being stolen from my checked luggage trumped any fear of TSA exposing the surprise. Thankfully, my carry-on bag went through the scanner without anyone deeming it necessary to investigate the contents by hand. We checked our other suitcases and had a smooth flight to NYC, where we stood by the carousel in baggage claim, anxiously waiting to see our luggage coming down the conveyor belt. After a sufficient amount of time passed for everyone else on our plane to retrieve their luggage, we were still without ours. The carousel abruptly stopped, and our bags were still nowhere to be seen. We proceeded to the airline counter and filed a claim for our missing luggage. The airline representative told us that the luggage would be sent them to our hotel room when it arrived later that evening. I was so thankful I had followed the leading of the Holy Spirit and hadn't packed the ring in my checked luggage.

As soon as we had checked into our rooms, Brooke wanted to go shop for some replacement makeup and toiletries. Shopping for replacement makeup was not on my list of priorities. I finally spoke up and said, "I want to go see the Rockefeller Christmas tree before we do anything else." I had held this big secret for so long, I could not wait any longer to ask her to be my wife.

I was a man on a mission. Hurriedly, I led the way to the monumental tree. As soon as we walked up to the tree, I got down on one knee, pulled out the ring, and asked Brooke to be my wife.

I know what you're thinking, "How James Bond of him!" She said yes as I put the ring on her finger. People around us started applauding, and Brooke asked someone to take a picture of us. It was perfect.

The perfect engagement ring became not so perfect when Brooke was pregnant with our son, Gabriel. Her feet and fingers swelled so much that the ring no longer fit. She did not want to have it resized, so she opted to buy a ring that looked similar but was what is called "fashion jewelry"—a nice way of saying "fake." She received so many compliments on her new ring. I could not help but think that if everyone loved this ring so much, I could have saved a lot of money and gone that route in the first place! After a couple of months, the replacement ring started to change colors and stain her finger, so she went back to the department store and bought another one just like it. This cycle was repeated four or five times.

Once Gabriel was born, I said to Brooke, "Please quit wasting your time and money on fake rings. Go get your real ring resized. We could have paid it off by now with the money we've wasted on imitation rings."

My point is this: whenever you settle for a counterfeit or an imitation, it will cost you in the long run.

SETTLING FOR A COUNTERFEIT

The spirit of Delilah can make us doubt our ability to hear God, causing us to question what God has spoken to us, and prompt us to romance things that bring destruction—counterfeits. Let's discuss further that word *counterfeit*.

The word *counterfeit* is defined as "forgery; something likely to be mistaken for something of higher value."[4] Some of the syn-

---

4. *Merriam-Webster*, s.v. "counterfeit," https://www.merriam-webster.com/dictionary/counterfeit.

onyms for *counterfeit* are "imposture," "fraud," "sham," and "fake." The enemy is all these things.

Jesus called Satan the father of lies. (See John 8:44.) Satan deceived one-third of the angels and caused them to be cast out of heaven. (See Revelation 12:3–9.) The first lie recorded in the Word of God, found in the book of Genesis, came from the mouth of Satan in the form of a serpent:

> *Now the serpent was more crafty (subtle, skilled in deceit) than any living creature of the field which the LORD God had made. And the serpent (Satan) said to the woman, "Can it really be that God has said, 'You shall not eat from any tree of the garden'?" And the woman said to the serpent, "We may eat fruit from the trees of the garden, except the fruit from the tree which is in the middle of the garden. God said, 'You shall not eat from it nor touch it, otherwise you will die.'" But the serpent said to the woman, "You certainly will not die! For God knows that on the day you eat from it your eyes will be opened [that is, you will have greater awareness], and you will be like God, knowing [the difference between] good and evil."*
>
> (Genesis 3:1–5 AMP)

Notice the deception that Satan used against Eve. He first made her question what God had spoken to them. "*Can it really be that God has said, 'You shall not eat from any tree of the garden'?*" The enemy wants you to doubt your ability to hear God's voice accurately. Eve then answered the serpent, "*We may eat fruit from the trees of the garden, except the fruit from the tree which is in the middle of the garden. God said, 'You shall not eat from it nor touch it, otherwise you will die.'*" The enemy slyly implied to her through his questioning that God was keeping something back from her and Adam. He planted the seed of the idea that they were missing out on something better than what God had already given them. He craftily placed the longing for the forbidden fruit in their minds.

The next step in his crafty deception was to directly oppose the consequences that God had given to them for disobedience. *"But the serpent said to the woman, 'You certainly will not die!'"* He still uses this method today in order to perpetuate the lie, keeping the church asleep in deception and defeat. He will shrewdly plant thoughts like, "I'm missing out on all the fun by living holy," "I'm not required to live a life consecrated to God," "As long as I am saved and headed for heaven, I'm good," or "The Bible is out-of-date. This is a different day." Many Christians yield to this way of thinking. They shape their foundation of faith on the lies and deceptions of the enemy.

The next ploy is the grandest of Satan's tactics. It is a lie that much of the church has unfortunately bought into: the lie that accepting things contrary to the Word of God will make you more like God. The serpent told Eve, *"For God knows that on the day you eat from it your eyes will be opened [that is, you will have greater awareness], and you will be like God, knowing [the difference between] good and evil."*

This is the bait that has captured much of the church in this hour. It is the foundation of the "woke" movement: greater awareness, more inclusivity, striving to make everyone happy, failing to confront sin, and classifying holy living as being bound to a spirit of religion. Our adversary knows the Word. He will twist the Scriptures to fit his agenda. This is precisely the reason that we are instructed to *"study to shew thyself approved unto God, a workman that needeth not to be ashamed, rightly dividing the word of truth"* (2 Timothy 2:15).

The "woke" church movement is the enemy's attempt to cause God's army to fall asleep by his deception. You can almost hear the hiss as he breathes, "You will be more like God if you accept everything that the culture of this world tells you is relevant." We must shake ourselves from these lies. The Bible, not the culture, is our standard. Again, we're taught in Romans 12:2:

> *Do not be conformed to this world [any longer with its superficial values and customs], but be transformed and progressively changed [as you mature spiritually] by the renewing of your mind [focusing on godly values and ethical attitudes], so that you may prove [for yourselves] what the will of God is, that which is good and acceptable and perfect [in His plan and purpose for you].*
> (AMP)

The word *"transformed"* in this Scripture is the Greek word *metamorphoo*, which means "to transform (literally or figuratively metamorphose), change, transfigure, transform." For me, the term calls to mind some toys that were extremely popular when I was a boy called Transformers. The appeal was that the toy would come packaged as one thing, but you could move their parts and turn them into totally different objects. A toy truck would convert into a robot. This is a picture of what God has ordained for His Word to do in the life of the believer. Your standard cannot be anything other than the Word of God. The progression that God ordained is for the believer to be *"transformed and progressively changed…by the renewing of your mind."*

> *And when the woman saw that the tree was good for food, and that it was pleasant to the eyes, and a tree to be desired to make one wise, she took of the fruit thereof, and did eat, and gave also unto her husband with her; and he did eat.*
> (Genesis 3:6)

A FALSE ROAR

The devil has a counterfeit roar. He is not a true lion. He releases a roar like a lion, but there is only one lion—the Lion of the tribe of Judah. (See Revelation 5:5.) Our adversary roams about attempting to intimidate us. He is looking to devour those who will cower at his threats. That is why the apostle Peter exhorts us:

Be sober [well balanced and self-disciplined], be alert and cautious at all times. That enemy of yours, the devil, prowls around like a roaring lion [fiercely hungry], seeking someone to devour. But resist him, be firm in your faith [against his attack—rooted, established, immovable], knowing that the same experiences of suffering are being experienced by your brothers and sisters throughout the world. [You do not suffer alone.] (1 Peter 5:8–9 AMP)

Notice that this Scripture starts with the command *"Be sober."* You must refuse to come under the influence of anything contrary to the Word of God. This can even include your favorite preacher or Bible teacher. Look past the gifting and examine the fruit. If there is strong gifting with little to no fruit, this is a sign of danger. It means that the person has honored their gift above the Giver of that gift.

It is easy for a person with strong gifting to move into a place where they rely solely on their gift and quit relying on God. We need to remember that every gift comes from God. He is the originator and giver of gifts.

Every good gift and every perfect gift is from above, and cometh down from the Father of lights, with whom is no variableness, neither shadow of turning. (James 1:17)

A remnant is rising that will resist Satan's temptation to taste the forbidden fruit, and I believe that you are reading this book because you are a part of that remnant. The army of God is awakening, firm in their faith and immoveable in their mission.

FALSE FRIENDS

As I began to relate this chapter to the life of Samson, the Lord revealed to me an essential truth that I had never seen before. God's chosen champion, Samson, habitually chose counterfeit relationships that consistently led to betrayal. This is how the enemy works, breaking down our resolve against his schemes little by little. Samson's first wife betrayed him at their marriage celebration over a riddle. I would dare to say this was not the first time she deceived Samson. Even after he knew that his wife had revealed the answer to his riddle to those who hated him and wanted to see him come to harm, he went after her, set on getting her back. She was like a magnet drawing him toward dysfunction. The enemy had carved an entry point in Samson's life. The worse women treated Samson, the more he desired them.

Most theologians believe that Delilah was a Philistine woman for a few reasons: (1) Samson was attracted to foreign women; (2) Delilah was from the Valley of Sorek (see Judges 16:4) in northern Philistia; and (3) the lords of the Philistines chose her to entice Samson. They most likely would not have tried to get an Israelite woman to betray her own people by delivering Israel's greatest warrior to the enemy, no matter the amount offered. Thus, it is safe to say that Delilah was almost certainly a Philistine. However, what intrigued me while writing this chapter is that Delilah is a Hebrew name that means "delicate, weak, languishing."

Why was a Philistine woman given a Hebrew name? Could it have been Satan orchestrating a plan, even to the detail of having her parents choose a Hebrew name? I am sure they did not know what they were doing when they decided to call their baby Delilah.

The enemy is strategic in his designs to stop God's people. Hell dispatches demonic spirits to study us and look for even the slightest weakness that they can use as a point of entry to fortify a stronghold in our lives.

This counterfeit woman had a Hebrew name but the cold hard heart of the adversary of God's people. The spirit of Delilah is not delicate, weak, or languishing. It is unrelenting, cruel, and deceiving. It is crucial that you stay alert, be on guard, and refuse to give place to the counterfeit spirit of Delilah.

AVOIDING COMPROMISE

The word *compromise* means "to make a dishonorable or shameful concession."[5] Compromise in the life of a man or woman of God is the enemy's playground. He rejoices with glee when a believer, who has been given authority over him and all his demonic underlings, makes concessions to him rather than binds him.

Samson was a Nazirite from birth, which meant he took the Nazirite vow and lived according to the regulations Moses outlined in the book of Numbers. The vow was threefold:

1. He would not drink wine or any strong drink. *"He shall separate himself from wine and similar drink; he shall drink neither vinegar made from wine nor vinegar made from similar drink; neither shall he drink any grape juice, nor eat fresh grapes or raisins. All the days of his separation he shall eat nothing that is produced by the grapevine, from seed to skin"* (Numbers 6:3–4 NKJV).

2. He would not cut his hair as a sign of his separation unto God. *"All the days of the vow of his separation no razor shall come upon his head; until the days are fulfilled for which he separated himself to the Lord, he shall be holy. Then he shall let the locks of the hair of his head grow"* (Numbers 6:5 NKJV).

3. He would not touch a corpse or carcass. *"All the days that he separates himself to the Lord he shall not go near a dead body"* (Numbers 6:6 NKJV).

I previously wrote about Samson's downward spiral as he continually broke his threefold vow to the Lord. Ultimately, he had played around with sin too many times until it overtook him. Once he opened his life to the spirit of Delilah, he would not be able to

---

5. Dictionary.com, s.v. "compromise," https://www.dictionary.com/browse/compromise.

shake off this concession that he had made to the enemy as he had done before. No! This time, his compromise cost him everything.

THE SPIRAL OF DESTRUCTION

Your adversary will endeavor to lure you into making concessions that seem very small and insignificant. He will convince you by whispering things like, "God does not care. No one will know. You will be fine." All the while, little by little, he is building a stronghold in your life. This was the pattern with Samson.

First, Samson decided to marry a Philistine woman, which was forbidden because she worshipped the false god Dagon. The text notes that when Samson was on his way to Timnath, most likely to finish the preliminaries for marriage to his Philistine bride, he went to the local vineyards. Why was Samson visiting the vineyards? The Nazirite vow forbade him from tasting even the skin of a grape. We see that one concession leads to another compromise, and on and on it goes. If Samson had not been set on marrying a pagan bride, he would not have been in the vineyards, where some suppose that he was tasting grapes or possibly even sampling a strong drink.

In these vineyards, a young lion roared against him. (See Judges 14:5.) This could be seen as an analogy to show the progressive pattern of sin. Remember the verse we examined earlier in which where Peter gave a firm warning comparing Satan to a roaring lion: *"Be sober, be vigilant; because your adversary the devil, as a roaring lion, walketh about, seeking whom he may devour"* (1 Peter 5:8).

God is rich in mercy, as demonstrated when the Spirit of the Lord came mightily upon Samson and enabled him to kill the lion with only his bare hands. Note, however, that Scripture says, *"But he told not his father or his mother what he had done"* (Judges 14:6).

Next, we read that Samson conceded yet again in his vow to God, continuing down the slide of compromise.

> *He turned aside to see the carcase of the lion: and, behold, there was a swarm of bees and honey in the carcase of the lion. And he took thereof in his hands, and went on eating, and came to his father and mother, and he gave them, and they did eat: but he told not them that he had taken the honey out of the carcase of the lion.*   (Judges 14:8–9)

Back in the vineyard, Samson looked for the lion's carcass and, upon finding it, saw that a swarm of bees had made honey inside of it. Samson took the honey with his hands and ate it. Take note that he both touched a dead animal and ate food that was considered unclean because it came from a rotting carcass. But it doesn't stop there. He also gave the honey to his parents to eat, again failing to reveal the full extent of his actions. Samson knew that if he revealed where the honey came from, he would expose his life of compromise. Samson's willingness to encourage his parents to eat something that was considered unclean reveals something of the condition of Samson's heart.

It seemed at this point that the enemy had convinced Samson that God was indifferent to his compromises, such as joining himself to Philistine women, drinking wine, and touching dead things. This is the method that the enemy uses to seduce believers into the spiral of destruction.

THE WATERS OF COMPROMISE

King David is another prime example of someone who dipped his toe into the waters of compromise and paid the price. David was at the wrong place at the wrong time. The Bible tells us that David was home in Jerusalem during the time of year when *"kings go forth to battle"* (2 Samuel 11:1). Take note that David was neglecting his assignment from God by not fulfilling his duty as a king.

And it came to pass in an eveningtide, that David arose from off his bed, and walked upon the roof of the king's house: and from the roof he saw a woman washing herself; and the woman was very beautiful to look upon. And David sent and enquired after the woman. And one said, Is not this Bathsheba, the daughter of Eliam, the wife of Uriah the Hittite? And David sent messengers, and took her; and she came in unto him, and he lay with her; for she was purified from her uncleanness: and she returned unto her house.   (2 Samuel 11:2–4)

The sad reality is that when you are distracted from your purpose, your destiny becomes sidelined. Satan will send distractions, whether by utilizing people, attacking the mind with wrong thinking, or making you feel overwhelmed. Today, entertainment is the premier distraction that your adversary sends against you. A small handheld device called a smartphone can steal hours, days, and even years as you simply scroll through news feeds and social media sites. I am not against technology. In fact, I believe that the apostles would have loved to have had today's technology and social media to use as a means of spreading the gospel. Yet your foe also loves it because it distracts you and steals time from you that you could be using to fulfill your kingdom assignment.

When David inquired about the bathing beauty, he discovered that she was the wife of Uriah. This did not stop David, for *"he sent messengers, and took her."* David compromised his walk with God and committed adultery. He desperately tried to hide his sin after learning that Bathsheba was pregnant with his child. He sent for Uriah to come home and tried to persuade him to spend time with his wife, but Uriah would not go because of his loyalty to his fellow soldiers and David himself. The king sent a letter to his commander Joab, ordering Uriah to be positioned in the fiercest part of the battle. Uriah's own king signed his death certificate.

And when the mourning was past, David sent and fetched her
to his house, and she became his wife, and bare him a son. But
the thing that David had done displeased the LORD.

(2 Samuel 11:27)

The escalation of sin in David's life can be clearly discerned. David was not fighting in the place of battle. He lusted after another man's wife, he committed adultery, he attempted to cover it up, and, when that failed, he arranged for her husband to be murdered.

I have heard it said, "When God desires to bless you, He will send a person into your life. When the enemy wants to cause you to stumble, he will send a person." Associations and relationships matter. The devil seeks to entangle God's children in wicked associations. He uses this tactic to keep believers tied up and distracted in order that he might corrupt God's plan for their lives. *"Be not deceived: evil communications corrupt good manners"* (1 Corinthians 15:33).

This was the same pattern we see in the life of Samson. Samson was called to be a deliverer of God's people from the oppression of the Philistines. Unfortunately, Samson was attracted to the very enemy he was to war against. His lust continually drew him into the land of the Philistines. This was a distraction from his God-ordained purpose. God, though, was merciful and turned it around for the good of His people, using Samson's wrong decisions to bring judgment against the Philistines. When Samson's wife betrayed him, he tied foxes together by twos, binding them together by their tails, placed a lit torch between their tails, then sent them out to burn the crops of the Philistines. After he fornicated with a prostitute in Gaza, the men of the city attempted to kill him, but their plan was spoiled when Samson tore the gates of the city and their posts and carried them on his shoulders. He thought he was unstoppable.

God is rich in mercy, but He cares more about an individual's soul than He does their outward gifting. God will always deal with you in private before He exposes your sin in public. At this point in his life, Samson was able to cast off God's conviction. He seemed to reason that the Holy Spirit would come upon him, and that his sin was not all that bad. And this is precisely how the enemy can entice anointed men and women of God to fall into his trap.

AVOIDING TOUCHING DEAD THINGS

When you became born again, you became dead to sin and are resurrected with Christ into new life.

Therefore if any man be in Christ, he is a new creature: old things are passed away; behold, all things are become new.
(2 Corinthians 5:17)

Your adversary desires for you to go back to demonic bondage. He does not want you to remain free. He will attempt to rope you once again in the chains that once kept you bound. He will present opportunities for you to "touch dead things" so that he might gain the advantage to overtake you.

Samson was so acquainted with handling dead and forbidden things that he had no resistance when it came to Delilah. The only part of his vow that Samson had not violated, which was also the secret to his strength, was that his hair had never been cut. His uncut hair symbolized that he had been separated unto the Lord. When the spirit of Delilah sought to destroy him, the first thing it attacked was his relationship with God. It was not after him to fornicate, for he had already done that. It did not entice him to drink strong drinks; he had already become familiar with the vineyards. Its lure was not to trick him into touching a carcass; once again, he had done it. This time was the strike of all strikes. This one would take Samson out to destroy his destiny. It came after his relationship with God.

The powers of hell desire to ensnare you back into the demonic chains from which Jesus has set you free. The devil is tormented when you live in freedom. Don't fall into his destructive web.

So if the Son sets you free from sin, then become a true son and be unquestionably free!   (John 8:36 TPT)

OVERCOMING SUICIDAL DEPRESSION

Suicidal depression is a symptom of the spirit of Delilah that most believers are unwilling to address because they fear being perceived as unbalanced or lacking faith. We know from statistics that this is a leading problem within the body of Christ. I recently read of a pastor of a large congregation who took his own life, leaving behind his wife and two small children. Sadly, we hear about these cases more and more often.

Suicide is one of the most devastating occurrences that can result from being attacked by the spirit of Delilah, and it makes me angrier at the devil than any other attack. In my previous book, *The Triple Threat Anointing,* I shared about my battle with depression. Since I'm intimately acquainted with the torment that the enemy uses to wear down a man or woman of God to be tempted to end the pain, my heart goes out to all those who face this dark attack of the mind. I encourage those of you who are facing this attack that God delivers and sets free. I know this because He set me free, and I'm walking in the joy of that freedom today.

Delilah's constant pressure had Samson wishing for death. Her words tortured him until he did not care if he lived or died. Words are extremely powerful to either build up or tear down.

A soothing tongue [speaking words that build up and encourage] is a tree of life, but a perverse tongue [speaking words that overwhelm and depress] crushes the spirit.

(Proverbs 15:4 AMP)

The great prophet Elijah also dealt with the spiritual symptom of suicidal depression after being mightily used by God to call fire down from heaven and bring revival to the people of Israel. The nation had fallen into an apostate condition after King Ahab of Israel married the Phoenician princess Jezebel. This wicked duo was responsible for the decay of God's people and the corruption of the country. Through their unholy alliance, they instituted Baal worship in Israel. Queen Jezebel was responsible for killing the Israelite prophets to eliminate those who would rival the influence of her pagan cult worship. The demonic spirits of Delilah and Jezebel operate similarly. They are both cunning, manipulating, and relentless.

The spirit of Jezebel attacked Elijah. Suicidal depression struck Elijah after he had called fire down from heaven, and the people of Israel fell on their faces and repented, declaring that Jehovah was the true God. King Ahab told Jezebel about what had happened and how the people obeyed Elijah's instructions to kill the 850 false prophets of Baal. She was full of fury, and the spirit that possessed her was out for vengeance. Jezebel sent a messenger to Elijah to relay her message that she was after his head. She swore that Elijah would meet the same fate that her false prophets had met. When Elijah heard her word curse against him, he fled.

Then Jezebel sent a messenger unto Elijah, saying, So let the gods do to me, and more also, if I make not thy life as the life of one of them by to morrow about this time. And when he saw that, he arose, and went for his life, and came to Beersheba, which belongeth to Judah, and left his servant there. But he himself went a day's journey into the wilderness, and came and sat down under a juniper tree: and he requested for himself that he might die; and said, It is enough; now, O LORD, take away my life; for I am not better than my fathers.

(1 Kings 19:2–4)

This text conveys how strongly this spirit attacks the true prophetic anointing after it is exposed. It also shows the effect its threats and curses can have against even the strongest of prophetic warriors. Elijah packed up and ran. This is precisely what the spirit of Jezebel desires to accomplish, even today, to ensure that it is left unopposed.

The Jezebel spirit thrives on intimidation and loves to silence the voice of the prophets. This demonic foe is not happy with just merely silencing the voice of the prophets. Its goal is to completely purge the pure prophetic. The Jezebel spirit has convinced individuals that they are the true prophetic voice.

Nevertheless I have a few things against you, because you allow that woman Jezebel, who calls herself a prophetess, to teach and seduce My servants to commit sexual immorality and eat things sacrificed to idols.   (Revelation 2:20 NKJV)

I wonder what would have happened if Elijah had remained with his foot on the accelerator of revival instead of going on the lam. He went from a fearless prophet, confronting sin and demonstrating God's power, to becoming full of fear and wishing for death. What happened? He faced the attack of suicidal depression. This is the same hellish attack Delilah used against Samson that had him broken and plagued with suicidal depression. Word curses, accusations, manipulation, and threats drove Samson to hopeless despair.

Although the church has been sometimes uncomfortable with addressing this subject, it must be exposed as a possible outcome after an attack by the spirit of Delilah. After coming through my own personal battle with suicidal depression, I continue to share my testimony.

Sadly, it is still taboo in the church to speak openly about the subject. When I first started sharing my testimony, I had a very sweet and well-meaning elderly lady tell me that I might not want to speak so frequently about depression. She went on to say that people might still think that I have mental issues, and I would not want to discredit my powerful ministry. She was afraid that people might conclude that I was somehow imbalanced. I kindly but boldly told her that as long as there was breath in my body, I would continue to tell everyone how God had set me free, and that He could do the same for them. I have had the opportunity to travel the world and pray with people to be delivered from the grip of the enemy. Our ministry has had countless lives set free from suicidal depression.

> *And they overcame him by the blood of the Lamb, and by the word of their testimony; and they loved not their lives unto the death.* (Revelation 12:11)

Every spiritual symptom of attack by the spirit of Delilah must be confronted so that each one is overcome and conquered.

4

PRAYER UNLOCKS SUPERNATURAL DELIVERANCE

The goal of the enemy in this hour is to overwhelm you until you forfeit your inheritance. He tries to accomplish his vicious plan by any means possible. He uses a plethora of attacks to wear down the sons and daughters of God. You must be able to recognize when you are under attack. During opposition, the principal thing is to realize that knowledge is half the battle won.

Coming from a background of word-of-faith teachings, I, like many believers, understand the power of words. Oftentimes, believers do not realize there is a balance in all things, including their confession. For example, when a believer commits a sin, they are to confess that sin to God and ask Him for forgiveness. They shouldn't go around in a state of denial, saying, for example, "I didn't lie. I didn't get angry. I didn't sin." How can someone expect forgiveness if they can't be honest with themselves, honest with the person they sinned against, and, most important of all, honest with God? Those who do not understand the balance of confession will deny that they are even under assault. This is not wisdom.

While believers must never come into agreement with the adversary and his report, a believer should always be cognizant of the enemy's schemes and ask for prayer. When you are under attack by the enemy, it is crucial that you come into the prayer of agreement with other Christians.

One of the greatest resources you have is agreeing in prayer with other believers.

> *Again, I say to you, that if two believers on earth agree [that is, are of one mind, in harmony] about anything that they ask [within the will of God], it will be done for them by My Father in heaven.* (Matthew 18:19 AMP)

There is wonder-working power available to be released into dire situations to bring needed change when two or more come together and pray the prayer of agreement. Jesus boldly declared that when two believers ask the heavenly Father anything, according to the will of God, it will be done. This is amazing! Did you grasp what Jesus said? He said that if two of the Father's children come into agreement, the Father will honor what they have agreed upon, and the Father will do it for them! If only the children of God would agree in prayer and bombard heaven with intercession, many of the enemy's tactics would be foiled.

VEXING THE CHURCH

In the book of Acts, we find the people in the early church coming into agreement over Peter's imprisonment and pending execution. Acts 12:1 opens by offering readers some context:

> *Now about that time Herod the king stretched forth his hands to vex certain of the church. And he killed James the brother of John with the sword. And because he saw it pleased the Jews, he proceeded further to take Peter also.* (Acts 12:1–3)

The religious leaders of the Jews had an intense desire to stop the Jews from believing that Jesus was the Son of God. Their zeal had caused them to become bloodthirsty for the forerunners of the church. In their view, the church leaders were nothing more than blasphemous troublemakers who needed to be stopped at any cost. The Jewish religious leaders' intent was to make the church leaders' deaths a public example that would warn other Jews not to embrace Christianity. They hoped that the apostles' public deaths would impede the gospel from spreading any further. In their warped view, the more brutal the death, the better it was for their agenda.

The first martyr was Stephen; he died by being stoned to death. (See Acts 6–7.) Stoning was the traditional Jewish method of execution. According to the same passage from Acts, the second martyr in church history was James, whom King Herod ordered beheaded with the sword. Beheading was the Roman method for execution. The Jewish rabbis were thrilled to see the apostle James die in that manner because they considered it to be a disgraceful death.[6]

Verse 1 tells us, *"Herod the king stretched forth his hands to vex certain of the Church."* The Greek word for *"vex"* is *kakoo*, meaning "to injure; to exasperate; to make evil" and "to harm." This is a perfect description of the activity of the spirit of Delilah. Remember, the Bible says, *"[Delilah] pressed [Solomon] daily with her words… so that his soul was vexed unto death"* (Judges 16:16). The enemy's cunning plan is to exasperate you until you give up and surrender to his evil plot.

When King Herod saw that it was earning him popularity points with the Jews, he advanced" in his persecution of the church. His next step was to arrest Peter.

And when he had apprehended [Peter], he put him in prison, and delivered him to four quaternions of soldiers to keep him;

---

6. *Dake's Annotated Reference Bible*, 136.

intending after Easter to bring him forth to the people.
(Acts 12:4)

Can you imagine what Peter must have thought as he was arrested and taken into custody? After Peter denied the Lord, Jesus comforted him and told him that there would come a day when he, indeed, would die for Him. (See John 21:18–19.) Peter must have wondered, "Is this it? Is this what Jesus was talking about? He said my hands would be bound and I would be led to my death. This must be my time to glorify His name." I can imagine his thoughts spinning with a strange mix of emotions, on the one hand looking forward to seeing Jesus, counting it an honor to die for the One who selflessly gave His life for all of humanity, and on the other hand considering what his death would mean for the church, which was still in its infancy. The glaring fact that James had just been executed did not escape his mind for one moment. Peter's steadfast faith and unwavering love for the Son of God governed him to reject fear of the cruel pain that he would most assuredly endure. He embraced the cost of being martyred for his resolute faith in Jesus. He had denied Him before, but he would not do so this time.

Peter was forcefully taken to his place of confinement, a dark jail cell. He was not treated as an average prisoner. The ambition of an insecure Roman leader who would do anything to keep control over his territory, along with the burning hate of the Jewish leaders for those who had believed in Christ, was ever present. King Herod assigned sixteen soldiers to rotate and personally guard Peter, a lone man. Peter was chained between two soldiers at all times to ensure that he could not escape. Peter's situation appeared to be completely hopeless.

OUT OF FAITH AND INTO FEAR

The harrowing situation in which Peter and the people of the early church found themselves is a graphic illustration of how the enemy is still working against you today. First, he applies maximum pressure on your every side, refusing to let up for even a brief reprieve. Second, he hurls lies and threats at you, in an attempt to move you away from your position of faith. And, third, he terrorizes you through thoughts of distress, giving his best effort to move you into fear.

Why does the enemy want to move you out of faith and into fear? Faith pleases God, and it is impossible to walk with God without faith. The enemy cunningly strategizes to move you out of intimacy with your heavenly Father.

I saw this reality in a vision I received in which two opponents were pulling on a rope in an apparent match of tug-of-war. I heard the Lord say to me, "The rope is the Word that I have decreed over that individual's life." I now realized that Satan was pulling on one end of the rope, and his opponent was a believer. Both were pulling the rope with all their might. I noticed that, at times, the believer would slip, and Satan would gain ground. God said to me, "The enemy is trying to pull them over into the natural realm in order to steal their promise. As long as the believer stays in the Spirit realm, they will hold on to their promise, and all of heaven will back them up. I will dispatch warring angels on their behalf."

While I was still in the vision, I wondered why the believer would slip and fight in the natural. Didn't they know that they were winning as long as they stayed in the Spirit? From this vision, we learn that the enemy is after your word—the Word of God that was decreed over your destiny. Satan is after your faith in God, because the Word is the vehicle that faith rides in. *"So then faith cometh by hearing, and hearing by the word of God"* (Romans 10:17).

But without faith it is impossible to [walk with God and] please Him, for whoever comes [near] to God must [necessarily] believe that God exists and that He rewards those who [earnestly and diligently] seek Him. (Hebrews 11:6 AMP)

THE POWER OF AGREEMENT

Great revival is often birthed during times of adversity. I have often heard it said, "'There has to be a 'break' in order to get to the 'through.'" To reach a breakthrough, we will face circumstances whose sole purpose is to break us.

After Peter's arrest, the early church could have found themselves at a breaking point. Yet, although Peter was presumed to be as good as dead, the church began to pray. Acts 12:5 tells us, *"Prayer was made without ceasing of the church unto God for him."* The impossibility of the situation caused desperation within the soul of the church. They prayed *"without ceasing"* (Acts 12:5).

Acts 12:5 is the most important verse in this story. It was the key to Peter's breakthrough. Notice what it says: *"But prayer was made without ceasing of the church unto God for him."* Prayer still breaks through the most devilish of attacks, even defeating the spirit of Delilah. Prayer and intercession are the instruments that God uses to release awakening.

The narrative goes on to tell us that, just hours before Herod was to bring Peter forth to execute him, God orchestrated a supernatural intervention.

> *And when Herod would have brought him forth, the same night Peter was sleeping between two soldiers, bound with two chains: and the keepers before the door kept the prison. And, behold, the angel of the Lord came upon him, and a light shined in the prison.* (Acts 12:6–7)

Could it be that God was waiting for the prayers of His people? What if, today, God is waiting for you to cry out to Him on behalf of your family that is locked in the clutches of the devil? Satan may be telling you that it is over for you. In the natural, it may look as if he is right; you can't see any way out. But take courage, my friend!

God will make a way for you even where there seems to be no way. Hold on! The Lord has heard your cry!

THE POWER OF LITTLE FAITH

I've always been struck by the detail that while Peter was chained between two soldiers, knowing that he most likely would be sentenced to death, he still managed to sleep. Could this have possibly been a lesson that he learned from Jesus while they were in a boat in the midst of a storm, and all the disciples feared they were about to perish? Let's look at this story as it's recorded in the gospel of Matthew. The account begins like this:

> And when he was entered into a ship, his disciples followed him. And, behold, there arose a great tempest in the sea, insomuch that the ship was covered with the waves: but he was asleep. (Matthew 8:23–24)

In verse 24, the word *"tempest"* is translated from the Greek word *seismos*, which means "earthquake." This was not your normal thunderstorm. This earth-shaking storm caused the waves to completely cover the boat. Peter, James, and John were professional fishermen well-versed in the dangers of such catastrophic storms. The disciples were terrified, and with reason! Nonetheless, Jesus slept in the boat until He was awakened by His fearful disciples.

> And his disciples came to him, and awoke him, saying, Lord, save us: we perish. And he saith unto them, Why are ye fearful, O ye of little faith? (Matthew 8:25–26)

It is important to point out that Jesus did not rebuke the disciples for waking Him. He never chastised them for calling on Him for help. He asked them a question: "Why are you so fearful?" In other words, Jesus asked His disciples, "Why did you move from faith over into fear?" It is so profound to me that He never rebuked them for waking Him. He wants us to call on Him in times of adversity. He invites us to put a demand on His power, and His desire is that we would not give in to fear.

You may look at this text and think that Jesus reprimanded the disciples for having *"little faith."* I don't believe this to be the case at all, for their *"little faith"* could have carried them through this storm. Rather, He rebuked them for allowing the spirit of fear to take hold of them.

Indeed, Jesus taught on the power of *"little faith,"* or, as He called it, *"mustard-seed faith,"* in the story of the boy who had epileptic seizures. (See Matthew 17:14–21.) In this account, a demonic spirit had possessed the boy, causing him to have seizures, and it tried to kill him by throwing him into both fire and water. The boy's father asked Jesus to cure his son, explaining that Jesus's disciples had tried but failed. After Jesus cast the devil out of the boy, His disciples tried to figure out what they had done wrong.

> *Then came the disciples to Jesus apart, and said, Why could not we cast him out? And Jesus said unto them, Because of your unbelief: for verily I say unto you, If ye have faith as a grain of mustard seed, ye shall say unto this mountain, Remove hence to yonder place; and it shall remove; and nothing shall be impossible unto you. Howbeit this kind goeth not out but by prayer and fasting.* (Matthew 17:19–21)

Pay close attention to the reason for the disciples' failure to cast the devil out of this young boy. Do you see it? It was their unbelief. When they asked Jesus why they had failed to cast out the devil, Jesus didn't try to soften the blow of His answer. He didn't tell them it wasn't God's will for them to cast it out. He didn't say to them, "You don't understand it now, but someday you will." No, He boldly and clearly told them the truth, even if it hurt them: They could not cast the devil out of the boy because they had *no faith*.

Jesus took this opportunity to teach and train His disciples for their future ministry. He said to them, *"If ye have faith as a grain of mustard seed, ye shall say unto this mountain, Remove hence to yonder place; and it shall remove"* (Matthew 17:20). The mustard seed is considered the smallest seed to be grown in soil. If we possess even the tiniest fraction of faith, we can speak to mountains and command them to be moved, and they will move. Faith has a voice. The voice of faith will always speak. Fear also has a voice and will speak. What voice will you allow to speak through you?

OVERCOMING FEAR AND UNBELIEF

Since Jesus addressed the topic of unbelief, let's take a closer look at the subject. In the story of the boy who had seizures, we see that unbelief stands in the way of us experiencing God's divine intervention. If you truly desire to see God's supernatural power flow through you—and I believe that you do, since you are reading this book—you must deal with the debilitating spirits of fear and unbelief. They work in conjunction with each other, and they are epidemic in the church today.

Let's start with fear. Fear is a spirit. It is not a feeling. It can manifest through feelings, but it is a spirit at its root.

For God will never give you the spirit of fear, but the Holy Spirit who gives you mighty power, love, and self-control.

(2 Timothy 1:7 TPT)

It is clear that the spirit of fear does not come from God; it comes from the enemy. In fact, it stands in direct opposition to faith. When the spirit of fear is given free access to someone's life, it will choke the faith right out of them until it becomes the dominating force of their existence. Fear restricts the Holy Spirit's mighty power from flowing through us and even immobilizes our self-control.

I remember a time from my adolescence when I had a close encounter with the spirit of fear. When I was a child, my parents would not allow me to watch horror movies or go to haunted houses. They knew the power of the spirit of fear and taught me not to give it access to my life, even in jest. When I was a teenager, I attended a youth conference in Gatlinburg, Tennessee, with my church youth group. It was during Halloween season, and there was a haunted house there with people dressed up in all sorts of scary costumes. My youth group decided that this would be fun for us all to do. Feeling pressured into going along with them, I reasoned with myself, thinking, "How bad can it be? There will be little kids and their parents going in. I'm not going to allow any demons access to my life just by going into this silly haunted house." Yet when we arrived at the haunted house, I kept hearing the voice of the Holy Spirit saying, "Andrew, don't do this. You do not want to play around with the devil and demonic spirits. You have been taught better than this. You have seen people that were truly possessed by the devil, and it is not something for your entertainment."

It was a dilemma. I could feel the tug of the Holy Spirit telling me not to go, but I was trying to rationalize that the experience would be okay. After all, it was in the name of fun. When we walked up to the house, there were people dressed as zombies, witches, and corpses. The Holy Spirit plainly spoke to me and said, "Andrew, you are not to go in. It does not matter what anyone else thinks of you. Do not open yourself up to the spirit of fear." I told the rest of the group that I was sorry, but I could not go in. Some called me a chicken and a scared baby, but I knew the voice of the Holy Spirit, and I wanted to obey Him more than I cared about the opinions of the other kids in my youth group.

Most of my peers went into the haunted house. There were only a few of us who stayed outside. That night, one of the guys who had been assigned to my room had a nightmare and started screaming in his sleep. Immediately, I knew why he was having the nightmare. He had opened himself up to the spirit of fear by going inside that haunted house.

Demonic fear is not your friend, and it's not from God. You are called to be a mountain-moving person of faith.

AN OPEN DOOR

Let's return to the story of Peter. Remember, he was in prison, awaiting execution, chained between guards, when the Lord intervened. Read what happened next:

> *All at once an angel of the Lord appeared, filling his prison cell with a brilliant light. The angel struck Peter on the side to awaken him and said, "Hurry up! Let's go!" Instantly the chains fell off his wrists.* (Acts 12:7 TPT)

According to *The Passion Translation*, the Greek word translated *"struck"* was the same word used to describe how Jesus was *"struck"* for our sins in Matthew 26:31. Jesus was pierced in His side to awaken hearts to God. Peter was awakened by an angel who struck him on his side to arouse him from his sleep. Take note that when Peter was awakened, his chains fell off instantly. This can be a prophetic picture of what happens when you are spiritually awakened to God: the chains that used to bind you fall off.

Next, the angel gave Peter very specific instructions.

> *The angel said unto him, Gird thyself, and bind on thy sandals. And so he did. And he saith unto him, Cast thy garment about thee, and follow me. And he went out, and followed him; and wist not that it was true which was done by the angel; but thought he saw a vision.* (Acts 12:8–9)

Let's take a closer look at some of these instructions. I believe there is a wealth of prophetic symbolism in verse 8. The angel tells Peter to:

+ **"Gird thyself."** According to *Vines Expository Dictionary*, the phrase *"gird thyself"* means "literally, of 'girding' oneself for service, for rapidity of movement." It is used by Paul when he wrote, *"Stand therefore, having your loins girt about with truth, and having on the breastplate of righteousness"* (Ephesians 6:14). The words *"Gird thyself"* symbolize the belt of truth.

+ **"Bind on thy sandals."** The angel was instructing Peter to be prepared to move quickly. God was taking him somewhere. These words also symbolize the preaching of the gospel. *"And how shall they preach, except they be sent? as it is written,* **How beautiful are the feet** *of them that preach the gospel of peace, and bring glad tidings of good things!"* (Romans 10:15).

+ **"Cast thy garment about thee."** These words symbolize the putting on again of one's mantle.

We can tell from these instructions that Peter was expected to move with haste. Whenever God is moving you out of an old season and transitioning you into something new, there comes a temptation to believe that it will take Him a long time. The opposite is true. When God moves, He moves swiftly. You need to prepare yourself for His "suddenlies."

Verse 9 tells us that when the angel came to Peter in prison, Peter believed he was having a vision; he didn't think that it was happening in real time. This could be attributed to his having fallen into a deep sleep before the angel awakened him, or it might indicate that he felt it was too good to be true. Don't ever doubt God's power to deliver you. God can dispatch angels on assignment, even at the "last minute."

The angel led Peter safely past the first guard and then the second, ensuring that Peter would not be detected and that his release would go unhindered. When Peter and the angel reached the city's gate, it opened of its own accord. This was truly the first automatic gate opening in history, and it was operated by the power of God! God will supernaturally open the barriers that have been put in place to keep you out of the places He wants you to go. I prophesy to you today that God is opening those shut gates to you and bringing you through them! Your prayers have unlocked your supernatural deliverance. No longer will those barricades that have been designed to keep you out of your destiny stand shut to you. This is your time!

Suddenly, the angel vanished, and Peter came to himself. The text tells us, "That's when Peter realized that he wasn't having a dream! He said to himself, 'This is really happening! The Lord sent his angel to rescue me from the clutches of Herod and from what the Jewish leaders planned to do to me'" (Acts 12:11 TPT). He finally understood that what he was experiencing was not a dream or a vision. God had indeed delivered him from the grip of his adversaries and their expectations for his demise.

Anyone who has come against you and your purpose is about to be very disappointed because God is coming through for you. The very ones who rejoiced at your entrapment will suddenly realize that your God is a deliverer, and He is on your side.

LET GOD ASTONISH YOU

Scripture tells us that after being miraculously freed from jail, Peter went to the house of Mary and her son, John Mark, where the church had gathered together praying for Peter's deliverance. When he knocked on the door, a young girl named Rhoda came to answer it. She instantly recognized Peter's voice, which tells us that she was accustomed to hearing him teach and preach. Rhoda is believed to have been around twelve years old. What she did next was what any shocked and excited young girl would have done: she forgot to open the door! (I am well acquainted with the forgetfulness that sometimes accompanies youthful exhilaration because I have witnessed it in my ten-year-old daughter, Giuliana.) Instead of opening the door for Peter, Rhoda ran to tell the intercessors that Peter was standing outside at the courtyard door, while Peter stayed where he was and continued to knock.

Those who were gathered there accused Rhoda of speaking as a maniac. They believed that she had lost her mind. *"You are beside yourself!"* (Acts 12:15 NKJV), they said. But little Rhoda stood her ground, emphatically confirming that she had indeed heard Peter's voice at the door.

It is interesting to me that the gate of the city opened of its own accord for Peter, but the door to the place where the church had gathered was closed to him. You must keep the door of expectation open for God to move on your behalf when you pray. The Word tells us that those gathered at Mary's had been praying *"without ceasing"* (Acts 12:5) for Peter's release, but when the answer came knocking at the door, they accused the young girl who reported it of having lost her mind. God wants you to move out of doubt and into faith. Expect God to answer your prayers.

When they finally opened the door and saw Peter standing there, they were *"astonished"* (Acts 12:16). God wants to do the same for you! He wants to astonish you with His miraculous power today.

5

AGENTS OF AWAKENING

Anyone who knows me knows that one of my favorite men in the Bible is David. He was passionate in his worship. He was unashamed in his pursuit of God. I have written and preached about him many times. His life has impacted me more than any other in the Word of God (with the obvious exception of Jesus).

One day, I was praying in the Spirit while running on the treadmill, and I heard the Lord say to me, "I am raising up a new generation of Davids." I jumped off the treadmill and started to pray more earnestly to receive the complete revelation of what He was saying. The first thing that came to my mind was that God is raising up a new generation of worshippers. I got excited because I am a worshipper! But just as that thought crossed my mind, the Lord said, "Andrew, Davids are rising to awaken revival to My warriors."

AN OLD TESTAMENT PICTURE OF DEFEATING DELILAH

First Samuel 4 introduces us to the Philistines, the enemies of God's people. The Israelites' interactions with the Philistines were the thermometer that gauged the spiritual temperature of Israel. In 1 Samuel 4, a great battle took place between these two peoples: the Battle of Aphek. This battle revealed much about the state of the tribes of Israel, particularly the significant damage that the priest Eli's refusal to remove his sons from the priesthood had brought to the entire nation. This priest, the prophet Samuel's predecessor, had allowed his sons to corrupt God's people and lead them into sin. The Battle of Aphek climaxed with the ark of the covenant being stolen, Eli's two sons being killed in battle, and Eli falling to his death, thus fulfilling the prophecy that had been pronounced against this wicked priesthood. (See 1 Samuel 2:12–4:17.) This battle sets the stage, helping us to understand the people of Israel's spiritual condition at the time David entered the scene.

The corruption of the spiritual leaders resulted in the depravity of the people, as well as their king, Saul, who was anointed by Samuel several chapters later. (See 1 Samuel 9.) It wasn't long before Saul proved to be a disobedient king, and the Lord directed Samuel to the next king of Israel: David. First Samuel 16:13 records, "*Then Samuel took the horn of oil and anointed him in the midst of his brothers; and the Spirit of the LORD came upon David from that day forward*" (NKJV). The very next verse records, "*The Spirit of the LORD departed from Saul, and a distressing spirit from the LORD troubled him*" (1 Samuel 16:14 NKJV) because of his disobedience. The people would be forced to follow a leader who was utterly demonized. They had likely grown so accustomed to sin that they could not recognize that Saul was no longer anointed but controlled by an evil spirit.

In the subsequent chapter, 1 Samuel 17, the Israelites faced the Philistines in battle again. This is a story that many of us are familiar with, as it includes the battle of David and Goliath. When we hear the name David, we immediately think of him killing Goliath. The story of David killing the giant Goliath is so well-known that it is often mentioned in stories of underdogs achieving victory, from the realm of lawsuits to the arena of sporting events. What we don't recognize as often, though, is that David defeated more than one giant that day in Elah. He also defeated the giant of the spirit of Delilah.

A TORMENTED ARMY

First Samuel 17:3–4 sets the scene for us:

And the Philistines stood on a mountain on the one side, and Israel stood on a mountain on the other side: and there was a valley between them. And there went out a champion out of the camp of the Philistines, named Goliath, of Gath, whose height was six cubits and a span.

Picture the Philistine army spread out on one mountain, and the Israelite army spread out on another mountain, with a valley in between them. The Philistines were not in a staring contest. They were there for battle. (See 1 Samuel 17:1.) The giant Goliath would come out, morning and evening, to mock Israel's army and their God. Scripture tells us, *"When Saul and the Israelites heard this, they were terrified and deeply shaken"* (1 Samuel 17:11 NLT). A later verse records, *"As soon as the Israelite army saw him [Goliath], they began to run away in fright"* (1 Samuel 17:24 NLT).

This was the spirit of Delilah! Do you see the effect that it had upon God's people? The giant was relentless in tormenting God's army with fear. Day and night, Goliath derided them in the same way that Delilah had done to Samson *"when she pressed him daily with her words, and urged him, so that his soul was vexed unto death"* (Judges 16:16). The spirit of Delilah was manifesting itself through Goliath. Daily, this spirit pressed God's warriors, causing them to run and hide in panic and dread.

Whenever God's people are deceived out of their authority, it can be described as slumber. In other words, they were asleep under the influence of fear. They imagined utter defeat and there-fore hid while the giant gained a more significant inroad to defeat the army of Israel.

A HERO ARRIVES

It is at this point that David arrives on the scene. David—having been anointed but not yet crowned king—was sent to the battlefield on an assignment from his father, Jesse. He was told to bring his older brothers an ephah of corn, ten loaves of bread, and ten cheeses. (See 1 Samuel 17:17–18.) David was coming to be a blessing to his brothers—but what the Israelite army did not know is that he also came to be a blessing for the entire nation!

> *David left his things with the keeper of supplies and hurried out to the ranks to greet his brothers. As he was talking with them, Goliath, the Philistine champion from Gath, came out from the Philistine ranks. Then David heard him shout his usual taunt to the army of Israel....David asked the soldiers standing nearby, "What will a man get for killing this Philistine and ending his defiance of Israel? Who is this pagan Philistine anyway, that he is allowed to defy the armies of the living God?"* (1 Samuel 17:22–23, 26 NLT)

David, a young boy in the natural, heard and saw this great giant taunting and defying the army of God. Thank God that David was not intoxicated by the spirit of Delilah manifesting itself through the giant.

David had been sent on a mission by his father to bless his brothers, but his elder brother Eliab did not recognize his mission; instead, he resisted it and stood against him.

> *Now Eliab his oldest brother heard what he said to the men; and Eliab's anger burned against David and he said, "Why have you come down here? With whom did you leave those few*

sheep in the wilderness? I know your presumption (overconfi-
dence) and the evil of your heart; for you have come down in
order to see the battle." (1 Samuel 17:28 AMP)

There are times when your heavenly Father will send you to
help brothers and sisters in Christ who will not receive you and
even lash out against you. If you are going to do anything to further the kingdom of God, you must be prepared to be misunderstood, judged, and rejected. Resolve to fulfill God's commission
and not become derailed from God's purpose for your life by these
discouraging obstacles.

I find it ironic that Eliab said, *"I know your presumption (over-
confidence) and the evil of your heart."* He judged David's heart as
evil. Remember that God said, *"I have found David the son of Jesse,
a man after My own heart, who will do all My will"* (Acts 13:22
NKJV).

David did not let his brother's harsh judgment stop him. He
refused to be dissuaded and continued with the Father's business.
He bypassed his brother and went straight to the top.

*David said to Saul, "Let no one lose heart on account of this
Philistine; your servant will go and fight him." Saul replied,
"You are not able to go out against this Philistine and fight
him; you are only a young man, and he has been a warrior
from his youth." But David said to Saul, "...Your servant has
killed both the lion and the bear; this uncircumcised Philistine
will be like one of them, because he has defied the armies of
the living God. The LORD who rescued me from the paw of
the lion and the paw of the bear will rescue me from the hand
of this Philistine." Saul said to David, "Go, and the LORD be
with you."* (1 Samuel 17:32–34, 36–37 NIV)

David did not decide to face Goliath because of what he
would receive from King Saul. The reward was only a by-product

of David's true motive: to avenge the living God whom Goliath had taunted and defied. David had been righteously provoked by the deception and oppression of God's people by the slumbering Delilah spirit that operated through Goliath. God had sent David as an agent of awakening.

King Saul tried to arm David with his own armor: *"He put an helmet of brass upon his head; also he armed him with a coat of mail"* (1 Samuel 17:38). This is a prophetic picture of the previous generation attempting to force-fit the armor of the last move of God upon the new move of God. David recognized that this was not the way God would move through him. He cast off Saul's armor and went to the river to pick out five smooth stones. He knew the battle would be won by using that with which God had equipped him and with which he had proven results.

Never discount the thing your God has placed in your hand. Compared to King Saul's elaborate armor, David's sling and his stones looked silly, but God wanted to move outside of the past parameters.

David did not meander and wait for Goliath to come for him. He *"drew near to the Philistine"* (1 Samuel 17:40). He went in a forward motion speedily because he was on an assignment to bring down this spirit that had overtaken the warriors of God.

As David approached Goliath, he continued to prophesy his victory over the enemy. He did not waver. David understood that he was a catalyst of revival. He had been sent to defeat the mocking spirit of Delilah that had overcome God's people.

> *Then said David to the Philistine, Thou comest to me with a sword, and with a spear, and with a shield: but I come to thee in the name of the LORD of hosts, the God of the armies of Israel, whom thou hast defied. This day will the LORD deliver thee into mine hand; and I will smite thee, and take thine head from thee; and I will give the carcasses of the host of the*

Philistines this day unto the fowls of the air, and to the wild beasts of the earth; that all the earth may know that there is a God in Israel. And all this assembly shall know that the LORD *saveth not with sword and spear: for the battle is the* LORD'S, *and he will give you into our hands.* (1 Samuel 17:45–47)

Scripture records that after David slew Goliath, he *"ran, and stood upon the Philistine"* (1 Samuel 17:51). David ultimately stood on the very thing that had been such a monument of fear. His problem became his platform. In both the natural and spirit realm, David was elevated above Goliath as he stood on his corpse.

When David recognized the spirit that defied the armies of Israel, he went into battle mode. He confronted the spiritual deception that had infiltrated the people of God and ultimately cut its head off. This mighty act resulted in an awakening of the people of God, and Israel's army was mobilized. The scales of fear and cowardice fell from their eyes, and they *"shouted, and pursued the Philistines"* (1 Samuel 17:52).

RISE UP, DAVIDS!

Much of the church today is asleep, and the enemy's stronghold to paralyze and bring defeat is gaining strength. It is easy to surmise how and why this is occurring. We are inundated with the enemy's propaganda, resulting in the church forfeiting her authority in the hope of not offending anyone. The church has been told what she can preach and how she is supposed to think, thus making the Word of God to no avail. Delilah has left us with a "woke" church, devoid of power. It saddens me to see the giant of Delilah raising over the church in this hour.

Where are the Davids? It is time for the warriors of God to arise and hasten toward this spirit and bring it down. It is time for you to be revived and recognize this spirit. Child of God, you already have been promised the victory. You have the power to slay the giant called the spirit of Delilah! You have been called to be a deliverer to this generation. You are called to be an agent of awakening, taking down the giants of this generation.

6

COLD TO THE FIRE

While I was praying alone in the sanctuary of my church, the Holy Spirit moved me into a prophetic flow of worship. I began to ask the Holy Spirit to "break in with fire" as He did on the day of Pentecost. Over and over, I repeated my request until there was a sudden shift in me. The Holy Spirit suddenly came upon me and made Himself known in the room. I was the only one there praying. I began to pray in the Holy Ghost and cry out, saying over and over, "More, more, more."

I have discovered that there is always "more" of God. We must never allow ourselves to become complacent in our hunger for Him. In fact, while I have been writing this book, I have been stirred to burn for awakening, revival, and deliverance for the masses as never before.

The Lord began to show me that the spirit of Delilah is really a demonic haze of slumber in which the enemy desires to keep the church bound. The truth is that whenever you are lethargic, you lose your desire to pray, read your Bible, and go to church.

Could it be that you are going through the motions and mechanics of a life dedicated to God, yet you do not have any real expectation that change will ever occur in your life or in the lives of your loved ones? If so, I would exhort you to wake up and recognize that Delilah is on the prowl to cause you to become cold—or, at the very least, lukewarm—to the things of God.

It is time for you to get your fire back! I'm not talking about feeling a Holy Ghost chill bump now and then. No! I am speaking of you being marked by fire. One of the attributes of fire is that it spreads. It cannot be contained, especially when it is accompanied by wind. These are the two elements used to describe what God did in the Upper Room on the day of Pentecost. God's intent was never for the Pentecostal experience with the Holy Spirit to be limited to the apostles or even to the one hundred and twenty. No, He sent the Holy Spirit to baptize you with fire so that you may set this generation ablaze.

I have come to set the world on fire, and I wish it were already burning! (Luke 12:49 NLT)

Doesn't it excite you to know that God wants to fill you with fire and use you as the kindling that spreads His fire? I know that it excites me.

For the promise is unto you, and to your children, and to all that are afar off, even as many as the LORD our God shall call. (Acts 2:39)

HEARTS GROWN COLD

I remember attending a service one night after a long day at the office. I had gone to show my support, but my heart was not there. I was tired, hungry, and ready to go home. After the worship, message, and altar call, things were coming to a close, and I could almost taste the turkey sandwich that was awaiting me at home.

Then the speaker abruptly said, "I don't feel like the Lord is done tonight; I believe He has something more for us." A group of young people bolted to the stage with banners and flags as the music began to crank up again. I sat down in my seat with my arms crossed. I remember thinking, "This is too much. It doesn't require all this. I am ready to go home."

It was then that I heard the familiar voice of the Holy Spirit say, "You're jealous." His statement left me bewildered. I wasn't jealous! I was hungry and tired!

The Holy Spirit didn't stop there. He went on to say, "You are not willing to do what they are doing. You won't break open your alabaster box because of a turkey sandwich."

I remembered the story of the woman with the alabaster box who lavished her worship on Jesus. When the disciples saw her costly act of worship, they were indignant and called it wasteful. Can you imagine perceiving any act of worship for Jesus as a waste? The disciples had become casual with Jesus, and their hearts had grown cold. They valued the precious ointment in the woman's box more than they did the Son of God. I have read this story hundreds of times and condemned them for having this heart posture toward her act of worship. Sadly, my heart was in the same place as theirs had been. Upon realizing that indignation had filled my heart, I fell to the ground and asked the Lord to forgive me.

God moved mightily upon me that night. The Lord had chosen that service, with me at that altar, to release a prophetic word that would shift the trajectory of my life and ministry. Even as I write this, I can't help but wonder what other things I may have missed that God had for me because my heart had grown cold to the fire.

FALLEN ASLEEP

After the resurrection, Jesus appeared to five hundred of His followers and commanded them to wait in Jerusalem for the promise of the Father.

And, being assembled together with them, commanded them that they should not depart from Jerusalem, but wait for the promise of the Father, which, saith he, ye have heard of me. For John truly baptized with water; but ye shall be baptized with the Holy Ghost not many days hence. (Acts 1:4–5)

Jesus instructed them not to depart. The word "*depart*" was translated from the Greek word *chorizo*, meaning "to place room between, reflexively to go away, put asunder" and "to separate." In essence, Jesus was saying to the five hundred, "Do not allow separation to come between you and the promise of the Father. Don't miss out on what I have for you." He even told them it would only be a few days until this outpouring.

Yet, out of the five hundred people who heard and saw Him, only one hundred and twenty chose to go and wait in the Upper Room for God's promise. What happened to the other three hundred and eighty? Did they not believe Him? Had they grown apathetic to the Son of God? We can ascertain that they valued something else more than they valued what God wanted to do in them. Sadly, we are no different. What have we missed of God because we have grown cold to the fire or were simply tired of waiting?

We aren't told their reasons for missing the outpouring of the Holy Spirit, but I can imagine they weren't much different from the excuses that we hear today: "Little Tommy has to be at his baseball game," "I've worked all week and need sleep," "I can worship the Lord at my house; I don't have to be in a physical location to have church," "The cost of gas is too high for me to drive across town." The list goes on and on. Serving as a pastor as long as I have,

I've heard them all. Let me say this: I am not against baseball, resting, or worshipping the Lord online. I do all of those things—but I am against letting those be replacements for getting up, getting dressed, driving to a church where the Spirit of God is moving, and fulfilling your responsibility as a participant in a corporate body of believers. Your worship matters. Your voice matters. Your anointing matters. Never let the enemy convince you that you don't matter in the body of Christ.

The book of 1 Corinthians also speaks of Jesus's appearance to the five hundred. It states:

He was seen by over five hundred brethren at once, of whom the greater part remain to the present, but some have fallen asleep. (1 Corinthians 15:6 NKJV)

The phrase *"have fallen asleep"* is a Hebrew euphemism for death when referring to believers, as reflected in the alternative translation *"have passed away"* (see, for example, TPT). Yes, this phrase is speaking of believers passing from the earth, but I believe this can also be a picture of the lethargic Delilah spirit that you are studying in this book.

The three hundred and eighty who had not gone to the Upper Room—surprisingly, the majority of the five hundred—had fallen prey to the same spirit that Samson faced with Delilah. Their guard had been taken down, and their vow to God had become secondary to their fleshly desires.

IN GOD'S TIME

I sometimes think of the ones who missed the birthing of the church. Did they ever experience the fire of the Holy Ghost? The Lord has not informed us, but one thing I do know is that I don't want to miss my set time from God. What about you?

In the Greek language, there are two classifications for time: *chronos*, referring to chronological time, and *kairos*, referring to "a set appointed time." You are reading this book right now because you are in a *kairos* moment. God wants to awaken you from slumber. He is stirring your heart and preparing you for a fresh outpouring of His Spirit. He's saying to you, "Press into the more I have for you. Don't miss your 'Pentecost' moment!"

> *On the day Pentecost was being fulfilled, all the disciples were gathered in one place. Suddenly they heard the sound of a violent blast of wind rushing into the house from out of the heavenly realm. The roar of the wind was so overpowering it was all anyone could bear! Then all at once a pillar of fire appeared before their eyes. It separated into tongues of fire that engulfed each one of them. They were all filled and equipped with the Holy Spirit and were inspired to speak in tongues— empowered by the Spirit to speak in languages they had never learned!*   (Acts 2:1–4 TPT)

Take note that before the "suddenly" came for those in the Upper Room, there was a period of waiting. The same is true for you. There is always a waiting period before God releases the "suddenly" in your life. Know this: it is the Lord who determines the length of your wait. The psalmist David acknowledged this truth when he wrote, "*My times are in your hands*" (Psalm 31:15 NIV).

The wait is the instrument, it is the sifter that God uses to separate those who will receive the promise from those who will not. Pay close attention to how those in the Upper Room waited. They weren't binge-watching movies, wasting time until it finally happened. No! They were praying and contending for their promise. "*These all **continued** with one accord in prayer and supplication*" (Acts 1:14). Sometimes, the biggest secret to possessing your promise is not giving up but continuing in what God has instructed you to do.

Note as well that Jesus's early followers continued in *"one accord."* The image given here is of a musical chord, meaning notes in perfect harmony together. How did they continue and stay in harmony? Through prayer and supplication. They were contending in prayer until they received what had been promised to them. This is the same posture that you must have while you are waiting. Stay actively engaged during the wait.

My point is this—you can go to church, enjoy the music, and listen to great messages, just to go home and live in the same lethargic condition. Don't settle for warming yourself by the fire and living off someone else's heat! Refuse to settle for simply warming yourself by the fire. Let the fire of God get inside you. God wants you to be baptized with the fire of the Holy Ghost. He desires for you not just to have revival but for you to *be* revival. God wants you to be a carrier of revival fire, setting others ablaze everywhere you go.

FILLED WITH FRESH FIRE

The spirit of Delilah is a revival killer. Its goal is to cause believers to slumber. You can slumber while attending church. You can sleep while attending a prayer meeting. You can even doze while you read the Bible. And even though you do those things that are essential to your spiritual life, and even though you stay around the fire, unless you break Delilah's stronghold, you will not be filled with the fire.

The woman Delilah enticed Samson to reveal the secret to his strength. She craftily set him up to be vulnerable before her as she lured him away from his commitment to God. What are the enticements that the spirit of Delilah has used to cause you to draw back from the things of God? Have you felt that your fire has grown cold? If so, pray this prayer with me:

Lord, I ask You to break the enchantments of the Delilah spirit off my life. I ask You to fill me with fresh fire. I resolve that I will no longer be bound to confusion or complacency. I ask You to help me live awakened, revived, and filled with fire. Today, I renounce and rebuke every lie, entrapment, and word curse of the enemy, in Jesus's name!

7

DELILAH LOVES
THE POWERLESS CHURCH

I once went through three years of demonic depression after breaking my pelvis in a terrible car accident. I could not walk for one year. As I lay in bed day after day, unable to care for myself, the enemy started weaving his lies of deceit through my mind. He began by saying things like, "You're not good enough. Everyone else is better than you. Look at you; you can't even get to the bathroom by yourself. You are an embarrassment." Day after day, he continued to press me with his words. Then he started planting seeds like, "No one loves you. Everyone would be relieved if you just died. Why don't you just end your life? You will never have joy again in this life. It's too late to fulfill the plan of God for you."

These thoughts plagued my mind until I reached the point where I began to think of anything that I could take just to stop the pain and end my life. When I reached rock bottom and was about to commit suicide, God spoke to me through a line in a song, "There's no God like Jehovah." That line jolted my spirit, and I cried out to God. His presence filled the room and totally set me free. I have never been the same since. I know firsthand how that spirit will press believers until their soul wishes for death.[7]

GNAWING AWAY

The enemy's primary tactic is to place you in a comatose, lethargic, and slumbering condition. He devises to disarm the warrior bride and leave her powerless against his demonic agenda. Why would soldiers at war lay down their weapons and seek comfort from their enemy? How does he do this? The enemy is cunning and strategic. He uses lies and propaganda to achieve his mission.

> *Ye are of your father the devil, and the lusts of your father ye will do. He was a murderer from the beginning, and abode not in the truth, because there is no truth in him. When he speaketh a lie, he speaketh of his own: for he is a liar, and the father of it.*   (John 8:44)

The Greek word translated "*devil*" is *diabolos*, meaning "false accuser" or "slanderer." The Aramaic word translated "*devil*" is *akelqarsa*, or "adversary," and is taken from a root word that means "to ridicule" or "to gnaw."[8] How do we define "gnaw"? It means "to bite or chew, especially persistently, to wear away or remove by persistent biting or nibbling, to form or make by so doing: to waste or wear away; corrode; erode."[9]

The Delilah spirit gnaws on God's warriors until they finally reach a place of surrender. It uses lies and manipulation to seize control of even the strongest of believers. The demonic spirit that controlled the woman Delilah used this manipulation method to break down Samson's defenses.

---

7. I wrote about this experience more fully in my previous book, *The Triple Threat Anointing*.
8. See John 8:44, footnote a, in *The Passion Translation*.
9. Dictionary.com, s.v. "gnaw," https://www.dictionary.com/browse/gnaw.

And it came to pass, when she pressed him daily with her words, and urged him, so that his soul was vexed unto death.... (Judges 16:16)

Delilah pressed Samson daily with her words. This spirit is unrelenting and will not be satisfied until it gains domination over God's people. It searches for a point of entry so that it can pounce and leave a trail of destruction in its wake. Delilah gnawed away at Samson's defenses with her lies of deception. She applied constant pressure to achieve her goal of wearying him. The pressure was intolerable until Samson wanted to die. He guarded neither his vow as a Nazarite to God nor his destiny. He did not care. He wished to die.

Whoever came up with the old saying, "Sticks and stones may break my bones, but words will never hurt me," did not understand the power of words. Words *will* hurt you, and the enemy knows that words can be used as a potent weapon against you to bring you to defeat.

A thief has only one thing in mind—he wants to steal, slaughter, and destroy. But I have come to give you everything in abundance more than you expect—life in its fullness until you overflow! (John 10:10 TPT)

Notice that the above Scripture says that *"he wants to,"* meaning this is Satan's desire. His desire is to steal, slaughter, and destroy you. The good news is that he cannot do it just because he wants to do it! Take a closer look at the statement Jesus made: *"But I have come."* That little phrase is so powerful. The fact that Jesus came cancels out the plot of the thief. The only way that the enemy can steal, slaughter, and destroy is if we grow weary and forfeit. The fact that Jesus came cancels out his plan.

CALLED TO BE DIFFERENT

Another way the adversary manipulates the people of God to lay down their spiritual arsenal voluntarily is by getting them to buy the lie that they can win more people to God if they fit in and are accepted, even admired, by the world. I have seen strong believers and God-fearing leaders be lulled to sleep by believing the lie that acting more like the world and making their services more palatable to worldly appetites will help them win more souls. Wake up! If you buy this lie, you have laid down your weapons and laid your head in Delilah's lap!

The church is called to be different. We are to be ambassadors of a different kingdom. Jesus was a friend of sinners not because He accepted their sins or joined in their behaviors. No, He found them in their sin and set them free from it. While it is true that He did not condemn the woman who was caught in the act of adultery (see John 8:3–13), He did, however, confront the sin. He told her, *"Go, and sin no more"* (John 8:11). If preachers are unwilling to speak out against sin, there will never be true repentance. If believers are reluctant to address sin or confront head-on the spirit of Delilah for fear of rejection, then their blood will be upon our hands.

> *But how can they call on him to save them unless they believe in him? And how can they believe in him if they have never heard about him? And how can they hear about him unless someone tells them?* (Romans 10:14 NLT)

As a young boy, I was overweight. How I wished to crave healthy foods instead of junk food! It wasn't until my teenage years that I became serious about changing my eating habits, and the result was that I lost one hundred pounds. I had to train my appetite to hunger for healthier food. I observe that many Christians are satisfied with religious "junk food" that possesses no spiritual nutrition. Our evil opponent has sneakily stirred a longing in today's church to be accepted by pop culture while shunning the moves of the Holy Spirit. Yet revival is birthed by the hunger pangs of those who want more of God. We must be filled with the same radical pursuit of Him that caused the apostles to turn the world upside down. They healed the sick, cast out devils, and preached the gospel with boldness. They were not afraid of rejection or of being misunderstood. They esteemed it an honor to be persecuted for Jesus.

What if Peter had preached a nice, feel-good message to the crowd on the day of Pentecost? I do not believe that a sugarcoated word would have *"pricked their hearts"* (Acts 2:37). No, Peter preached the truth. He confronted their sin, and their response was, *"What shall we do?"* (Acts 2:37).

> *Peter replied, "Repent and return to God, and each one of you must be baptized in the name of Jesus, the Anointed One, to have your sins removed. Then you may take hold of the gift of the Holy Spirit. For God's promise of the Holy Spirit is for you and your families, for those yet to be born and for everyone whom the Lord our God calls to himself." Peter preached to them and warned them with these words: "Be rescued from the wayward and perverse culture of this world!"*
> (Acts 2:38–40 TPT)

Peter used strong words to deliver a pointed message. Acts 2:41 tells us how his message was received: *"Those who believed the word that day numbered three thousand. They were all baptized and added to the church"* (TPT). Only the power of the Holy Spirit can cause three thousand people to repent and be baptized.

What if Paul had placated the people in the territories where he had been sent? What if Jesus had not cast out devils and healed the men with leprosy? That is not the gospel. We must sound the alarm and rouse God's army from sleep.

*The apostles left there rejoicing, thrilled that God had consid-
ered them worthy to suffer disgrace for the name of Jesus.*
(Acts 5:41 TPT)

Today, I ask you: Are you striving to fit in where you have
been called to stand out? Break free from the demonic agenda that
would silence your voice. You are God's champion.

UNDERCOVER CHRISTIANS

Have you ever noticed that society, for the most part, is okay
with your being a believer as long as you look like them, sound
like them, and think like them? Sad to say that a large portion
of Christians easily fit into this mold. I call them "undercover
Christians." They are so undercover that no one knows they are
Christians at all. If you keep your faith, beliefs, and values to
yourself, you're accepted. The world seethes with accusations of
Christians being intolerant, all the while exhibiting glaring hypoc-
risy as they are intolerant of those who believe the Bible and live
their life accordingly.

This was the scheme used by the woman Delilah against
Samson, the Nazarite. The spirit of Delilah is positioning herself
in direct opposition to a genuine move of the Holy Spirit by offering a counterfeit trend as a new option. Good-hearted people are
currently deceived by this brand of Christianity that is nice and
inoffensive but transparently devoid of power.

The apostle Paul wrote a letter to his spiritual son, Timothy,
warning him of the evil that would take place in days to come:

*But you need to be aware that in the final days the culture
of society will become extremely fierce. People will be self-cen-
tered lovers of themselves and obsessed with money. They
will boast of great things as they strut around in their arrogant pride and mock all that is right. They will ignore their*

own families. They will be ungrateful and ungodly. They will become addicted to hateful and malicious slander. Slaves to their desires, they will be ferocious, belligerent haters of what is good and right. With brutal treachery, they will act without restraint, bigoted and wrapped in clouds of their conceit. They will find their delight in the pleasures of this world more than the pleasures of the loving God. They may pretend to have a respect for God, but in reality they want nothing to do with God's power. Stay away from people like these!

(2 Timothy 3:1–5 TPT)

In the *Amplified Version*, verse 5 reads, "*Holding to a form of [outward] godliness (religion), although they have denied its power [for their conduct nullifies their claim of faith].*"

Paul wrote that there would be *"perilous times"* (2 Timothy 3:1), describing how the church would embrace a form of outward godliness (religion) but deny its power. In other words, they would embrace calling themselves Christians but reject the power of God to transform them. Paul described a people that would cast off the manifestations of the Spirit of God. Why would anyone settle for passionless worship and sugarcoated words? They would if they had been deceived. Such people have been captured by the wiles of the spirit of Delilah.

HUNGRY FOR GOD

One day, while I was praying in the Spirit, I went into a vision in which I saw a child's play kitchen with pots and pans, appliances, and even groceries. This vision was detailed, and it looked exactly like an actual, beautiful, state-of-the-art child's kitchen. It was then that the Lord revealed to me that it was a kitchen meant for small children but made to look extremely realistic. The Holy Spirit spoke to me and said, "My church has been satisfied with pretend food and play kitchens. It looks good, but it is not real.

There is no power. The stove and oven have no fire. There is no cur-rent of electricity to give it power. It is useless. It looks pretty, but it has no power. Play time is over! I am visiting My church with real fire and filling them with genuine Holy Ghost power. I will feed those that will hunger for Me, and they will be satisfied."

Hunger and desire are key ingredients to experiencing, individ-ually and corporately, a move of God's Spirit. The spirit of Delilah will try to satisfy your hunger by distraction. I often say that you hunger for what you feed on. If you feast on dead or fleshly things, those will be the things that your appetite will crave.

Samson had an appetite for things that went against his vow as a Nazarite. He gave way to behavior that became a pattern of com-promise. These acts became what he craved. His indulgence for sin led him to Delilah, and she would become his ultimate downfall.

The enemy uses the same spirit of Delilah today, as he did with Samson, to lull the church into a mindset prone to deception that easily accepts a sham version of Christianity. In his final epistle, believed to have been written between AD 66 and 67, Paul revealed that the imitation of God's power within His collective people is nothing new.

In the last days dangerous times [of great stress and trou-ble] will come [difficult days that will be hard to bear]. For people will be lovers of self [narcissistic, self-focused], lovers of money [impelled by greed], boastful, arrogant, revilers, dis-obedient to parents, ungrateful, unholy and profane, [and they will be] unloving [devoid of natural human affection, calloused and inhumane], irreconcilable, malicious gossips, devoid of self-control [intemperate, immoral], brutal, haters of good, traitors, reckless, conceited, lovers of [sensual] plea-sure rather than lovers of God, holding to a form of [outward] godliness (religion), although they have denied its power [for their conduct nullifies their claim of faith]. Avoid such people and keep far away from them. For among them are those who worm their way into homes and captivate morally weak and spiritually-dwarfed women weighed down by [the burden of their] sins, easily swayed by various impulses, always learning and listening to anybody who will teach them, but never able to come to the knowledge of the truth. Just as Jannes and Jambres [the court magicians of Egypt] opposed Moses, so these men also oppose the truth, men of depraved mind, unqualified and worthless [as teachers] in regard to the faith.

(2 Timothy 3:1–8 AMP)

We are living in the times that Paul wrote about here. We can see this today all over the world. I have experienced this firsthand when I have had pastors say to me, "If you want to see growth in your church, you'd better tone things down and become more seeker friendly." Tone things down? No, I am getting ready to amp things up. King David did not tone things down when his wife, Michal, criticized his extravagant worship. No! He became even more undignified. I ask the question of them, "Leaders, who are you seeking: people or God?"

The phrase *"having a form of godliness"* in 2 Timothy 3:5 is translated from the Greek word *morphosis* and means "formation," "appearance," "semblance," "sketch," or "form." The word *"power"* in this verse is *dunamis*, defined as "inherent power, power residing in a thing by virtue of its nature, or which a person or thing exerts and puts forth." The same Greek word is used in Acts 1:8:

But ye shall receive power, after that the Holy Ghost is come upon you: and ye shall be witnesses unto me both in Jerusalem, and in all Judaea, and in Samaria, and unto the uttermost part of the earth.

This verse follows Jesus's command to His followers to wait in Jerusalem for the promise of the Father (see Acts 1:4), which was the baptism of the Holy Spirit. Notice that He communicated to the early church their need for the power of the Holy Spirit to be witnesses for Him. If they needed Holy Ghost power to build the New Testament church, how much more do we need the Holy Spirit's power today?

Church, it's time to wake up. Larry Sparks teaches,

What will awaken a generation that's sleeping in on Sunday? The Supernatural. A Kingdom that moves and advances with power! When Jesus enters in and turns the tables of comfortable Christianity, all bets are off, and decently and in order looks more like the book of Acts than a tightly choreographed Broadway production.[10]

The counterfeit church stands in direct opposition to the awakened, revived, power-filled church. Production cannot be a replacement for God's presence. There is no substitute for His presence.

PURSUE PURITY

I have been ministering since I was eight years old. I started traveling and ministering at the age of twelve. I have seen a lot of junk and a lot of purity. I look back in amazement at how the Lord guarded my innocence. He surrounded me with ministers who were pure in heart—genuine men and women of God who showed me how to walk with God in purity.

However, I sometimes encountered ministers who did not live out what they preached. When I was twelve years old, I was singing at a conference where the guest minister preached a message on salvation. Hundreds of people rushed to the altar to give their hearts to Jesus. Sadly, I soon discovered that this man was not living offstage what he preached onstage. I was so disappointed, and I was left feeling very confused. I thought to myself, "How

---

10. Larry Sparks, text correspondence with author.

can this minister preach the Word of God and have hundreds of people give their lives to Jesus, while he is not living a holy life?"

The presence of God is holy. His presence cannot be mixed with sin. To have the manifestation of the presence of God, there must be righteousness and purity.

> *Who, then, is allowed to ascend the mountain of Yahweh?*
> *And who has the privilege of entering into God's Holy Place?*
> *Those who are clean—whose works and ways are pure, whose*
> *hearts are true and sealed by the truth, those who never deceive,*
> *whose words are sure. They will receive Yahweh's blessing and*
> *righteousness given by the Savior-God. They will stand before*
> *God, for they seek the pleasure of God's face, the God of Jacob.*
> *Pause in his presence.*   (Psalm 24:3–6 TPT)

This is why we cannot be so impressed with gifting that we overlook character and purity. Gifting is a gift. Holiness and purity are found in the pursuit of God and in the process of being transformed by His power. I am more impressed by someone who has consistently walked with God and lives for Him than I am with someone who can preach a dynamic message or sing the wallpaper off the wall.

God wants to refill you with His power today. You were not made to live in hollow Christianity. No! You are God's chosen vessel. You are a joint-heir with Christ. Today, refuse to allow Delilah to render you powerless. You have the Holy Spirit, and He is your Source of power.

8
FRESH OIL FROM A NEW CONTAINER

The enemy is a master manipulator. He loves to trap believers in their past so that they never move into their future. He tempts them to romance their past. He floods their thoughts with pleasant memories that trigger them to get stuck in what was. This is one of the most common tools that the enemy will use to stop believers from stepping into their destiny.

The children of Israel fell into this trap when, after being led into freedom by Moses, they began to long for the abundance of food they had enjoyed while enslaved in Egypt. *"We remember the fish, which we did eat in Egypt freely; the cucumbers, and the melons, and the leeks, and the onions, and the garlic"* (Numbers 11:5). They did not reason that Egypt was no longer the same place where they once had lived. When they left, they had stripped Egypt of its treasures and riches. God had destroyed the former glory of Egypt with His ten plagues. Egypt's bountiful food supply was no more. There were no longer men to work the fields. They did not reason that Pharaoh and his men had been drowned in the Red Sea while pursuing God's people during their miraculous exodus from Egypt. God made sure that they would never return to what used to be. They had been delivered from their past! He said to them, *"I am the* LORD *thy God, which have brought thee out of the land of Egypt, out of the house of bondage"* (Exodus 20:2).

God has brought you, too, out of your past, the house of bondage. Quit romancing it! If you find yourself longing for times gone by, you are falling into the enemy's strategic plan to keep you from reaching what God has promised you. Your best days are still ahead of you. The apostle Paul wrote to the believers in the Philippian church regarding freeing themselves from the past. He shared with them what he had put into practice in his own life. You, as a believer, must look forward to what is to come and not backward to what used to be!

> *Brethren, I count not myself to have apprehended: but this one thing I do, forgetting those things which are behind, and reaching forth unto those things which are before, I press toward the mark for the prize of the high calling of God in Christ Jesus.*
> (Philippians 3:13–14)

Paul was locked in a prison when he wrote those words. If anyone had a right to be reflecting wistfully on the past, it was he! Nonetheless, Paul stressed the importance of forgetting what once was and reaching for what is to come. In essence, he said there is more ahead for you; that your life's story is not over. Close the chapter on the past. The book of your life is not finished. The end of your story has not been told. As long as there is breath in your body, God has a plan for you.

You must live your life as if you are running in a race. You cannot afford to waste another moment doing anything besides pressing toward the finish line. When Paul said in verse 14, *"I press toward the mark for the prize,"* he was using the metaphor of an athlete striving for a prize. Press forward to what lies ahead. You cannot run a race looking backward. No one can if they want to win the race! A runner's eyes must be looking forward to what is ahead. You may have to press through hurt, you may have to press through rejection, you may have to press through broken dreams, but know this: at the end of all your pressing through, a prize awaits you, and you will rejoice, saying it was worth it all. Jesus is worth it all.

PRESSING FORWARD

I was very close to my mom's parents growing up. We lived down the street from them, and I would go to their house every day. My grandfather was kind and generous, as well as a very wise and successful businessman, but he lacked one thing: he was not born again. Nevertheless, he was what many would refer to as a "good man," meaning he would bend over backward to help someone in need. I loved going to see my granddad. Many people considered him gruff, and he smoked his cigars like a chimney, but I saw no fault in him. I loved being with him.

My granddad spoiled me in a lot of ways. There were really no rules for me to follow at his house. He would often wake me from sleep to have a midnight snack with him, usually consisting of a grilled cheese sandwich or some ice cream. (It was seldom a nutritious snack.) Granddad was also adventurous and a lot of fun to be around. He owned a helicopter, and there were many occasions when we would drive to the airport and fly over the city in the middle of the night. Spending time with my granddad was truly every young boy's dream.

My grandmother, a godly woman, was beautiful inside and out. Starting when she was a child and continuing even into her later years, people would stop her to ask if she was a movie star. She exuded class in everything she did. The funny thing was that she had not been raised with wealth or privilege. Her beginnings were quite humble. She was the eldest of seven children born on a small working farm. Grandmom was raised in meager and unfortunate circumstances and had to work in a broom factory as a young child to help support her family. This experience contributed to her industrious work ethic and resulted in her becoming a successful businesswoman in her own right. Grandmom was also a powerful intercessor. We would frequently go to her guest room, which was located above the garage, and pray. I can still hear the sound of her voice as she prayed in the Spirit while I lay on the floor beside her, also praying.

As I said earlier, my granddad was not born again when I was growing up. Even so, he was interested in the things of the Lord. We always listened to televangelist Jimmy Swaggart's music when we rode in his car. He would also watch Jimmy's telecast and cry during the entire sermon.

At some point, I became aware that my granddad had not received Jesus as his Savior. From that time on, I would wait for him to come home from work every afternoon, and as soon as he pulled his car into the driveway, I would ride my three-wheeler to his house. I would stand in front of his television set, even while he was trying to watch it, and sing every gospel song that I knew. I would then give an altar call, asking if he was ready to receive Jesus in his heart. Every day, I believed that would be the day he would pray the sinner's prayer with me.

He never responded to the call. Frustrated that his heart was not moved by my attempts to get him saved, I would stomp off into another room, and he would laugh—but not in a cruel way. He took joy in seeing my passion for the things of God and in witnessing the deep care I had for his soul.

When I was four years old, I received the baptism of the Holy Spirit. The excitement of receiving my prayer language propelled my zeal for God more than ever before. I had always been bold about my faith; however, being filled with the Holy Ghost took my boldness to another level, even at four years old!

After this momentous encounter with God, my mother and I joined my grandparents for a trip to Los Angeles, California. We stayed at one of the city's finest hotels. One day of our trip, my mother and grandmother went shopping, leaving me in the care of my granddad. I loved when it was just the two of us, for then I had his undivided attention. I preferred his company to anyone else's, but he sometimes struggled to keep up with the energy of an active four-year-old boy. Our hotel room was many floors above ground level, with a veranda encircling it—to me, the perfect platform for preaching to the masses of people passing by on the busy street below. This built-in stage was too great an opportunity for my childish mind to pass up, so I went out there and put on the best gospel performance possible. I sang. I preached. I prayed. I exhorted. I prophesied. I gave it my best. (I had a loud voice even back then!) I sometimes wonder what the other hotel guests thought of the little boy preaching at the top of his lungs from the veranda.

As soon as my mother and grandmother walked in the door after their outing, Granddad said to them, "I'm glad you're back. He's been preaching to everything that moves." Although he was joking, I could tell that my grandfather was proud of my determination to share the gospel with everyone I met.

A few years down the road, Granddad was diagnosed with cancer. On the day Granddad had surgery, his doctor took one look and then closed him back up. There was nothing he could do. Cancer had spread into his bones. Evangelist Jimmy Swaggart, by this point a family friend of ours, came to the hospital and led him to the Lord during that time. I was thrilled and sad at the same time. I was thrilled that he had accepted Jesus as his Savior. I was sad because a death sentence loomed over his natural body.

My grandfather, a giant of a man, had always seemed invincible to me. I struggled to accept the fact that he was in the hospital dying. He had been given only weeks to live. Our entire family began to fast and pray for his complete healing. Not long after this, my mother received a newsletter in the mail with the phrase "He shall live and not die and declare the works of the Lord" printed in big, bold letters. She knew this was God's answer on the matter.

That word proved to be truly prophetic. Granddad was eventually released from the hospital to spend his remaining days at home. At a follow-up appointment, the doctor realized that something had shifted in Granddad's body. He ordered new tests done. Additional tests followed. Finally, after all the tests, the doctor—who happened to be a close, personal friend of Granddad's—came to my grandfather, ecstatic, and announced, "The cancer has shriveled up in your body." Remarkably, those were the exact words our family had used when we would command, in prayer, "Cancer, shrivel up, in Jesus" name." Yes, all traces of cancer had miraculously left my granddad's body. It was a miracle! His healing did not come through surgery, radiation, or chemotherapy but by the hand of the Great Physician. The day that he received Jesus Christ completely changed his life, as did the day he discovered he was healed.

God used both my grandparents in mighty ways. They served as directors on the boards of many powerful and impactful ministries, imparting wisdom on business decisions that affected the world. I stand in awe of how God uses different talents and giftings to further the kingdom. My grandparents never stood behind a pulpit. They never preached a sermon. They never drew big audiences. But I can tell you, without a shadow of a doubt, that their work for the Lord has affected millions of souls.

Eighteen years after Granddad's diagnosis, on a Christmas Day, he graduated to heaven. I grieved the day that he went home to be with the Lord. I was at a restaurant in New York City when I received the news that he had passed, and the pain I felt was how I imagined it would be if someone stabbed me. It was a deep ache that I can't explain. I worried about who I would talk to when I had a problem. Who would listen to my future dreams? Who would support me in all my ministerial endeavors? Would there be anyone to fill the hole he had left in my heart? Grieving, I walked back to my hotel to pack my bags for home. As soon as I walked through the door of my hotel room, I fell to my knees, weeping. Right then, God showed me a vision of Granddad completely healed, dancing and leaping around the throne room. God spoke to me and said, "He is not in your past. He is in your future. He is now complete and whole and is experiencing realms of worship that you have only dreamed about." Hearing this assurance brought me such peace.

There are still days when a particular memory of Granddad crosses my mind, and I find myself reminiscing about our times together. I have come to realize that no matter how much I would love to go back to the days when I would sit on the sofa beside him in his recliner for a long heart-to-heart talk, God gave me that precious time for only a season of my life. He gave me that relationship in the past in order to shape my future. I can't go back. Things can never again be like they were. I am a grown man now, with children of my own. I serve as pastor to a wonderful congregation; I travel the world speaking at conferences. My cherished memories made with my granddad have molded me, shaped me, and added character to the man I have become. That was what God meant for them to do. We can never go back to the past. We have to progress forward. Granddad would have wanted me to continue moving forward, and I know my heavenly Father does not want me living in the past. He has called me to press toward the mark. He wants me to go from faith to faith and from glory to glory.

DON'T BE HELD CAPTIVE BY THE PAST

First Samuel 16:1 reveals how easy it is to be captured and held in the past. Even the great prophet Samuel was tempted to live in the state of *what could have been*. He wept over the one whom he had anointed to be king. He had opened his heart to Saul and had great expectations for him. How heartbreaking it was for Samuel when God decreed that the kingdom of Israel would be stripped from Saul due to his disobedience. God interrupted Samuel as he was grieving and asked him,

> *How long wilt thou mourn for Saul, seeing I have rejected him from reigning over Israel?*   (1 Samuel 16:1)

This verse conveys the depth of love that the prophet Samuel had for King Saul. He was in deep despair as he mourned what had been and what could have been. It was over. His great affection for Israel's first king and his hopes of him leading Israel in the ways of God were dashed with Saul's rebellion.

Samuel remembered Saul as he used to be. Saul wasn't always evil. Even though we tend to paint Saul as a wicked king who tried to kill his successor, David, the truth is that in the beginning of Saul's rule, he was anointed and used by God to bring about great victories for God's people. Unfortunately, many leaders today are like Saul, having started out with a pure heart and the motive to be used by God, only to have their heart corroded and their motives corrupted somewhere along the way. This was Saul's story. That is why we read of Samuel's grief over him.

But then God asked Samuel, "How long will you mourn for your past?"

Do you know that He's asking the same question of many of you today? At the same time, the Lord is prophetically announcing to you that there is a changing of the guard taking place for His people. A new shift is happening for you at this moment, taking you out of the old and bringing you into the new. A new season is upon you, as it was for Samuel and all of Israel. Even as there was a David waiting to take Saul's place as God's instrument of blessing to the entire nation, so has an instrument of blessing for you in this new season been prepared and set in order by God.

God did not wait for Samuel's answer. Instead, God proceeded to give him instructions: *"Fill thine horn with oil, and go"* (1 Samuel 16:1). In other words, "I am moving you out of what was and into what will be." God had found Himself a king among Jesse's sons.

FIND FRESH OIL

One day while I was on my way to church, I encountered a lane closure on the road where our church is located. The traffic was backed up and had come to a complete stop. As I sat there in my car, I noted a big orange construction sign. It read, "FRESH OIL NEXT 3 MILES." Immediately, God spoke to me that fresh oil would be poured out in our church. Now, some people might say that I was reading too much into a road sign. Yet I have learned that if we have our spiritual ears open for His voice, God will speak to us in a plethora of ways.

The oil spoken of in the Bible, used for spiritual and practical purposes, was olive oil. The olive tree and its oil have been prominently featured in the culture and rituals of Israel. Its great value is realized by the numerous verses that mention it in the Old Testament. In biblical times, the various uses of olive oil included cooking, medicine, and light. *"And thou shalt command the children of Israel, that they bring thee pure oil olive beaten for the light, to cause the lamp to burn always"* (Exodus 27:20).

Most notably, though, oil was a picture of the Holy Spirit and His anointing. Kings, priests, and prophets were all anointed with oil as an outward sign of their consecration for a holy purpose. For example, Saul was anointed with oil before becoming king of Israel.

Before we can fully understand the metaphorical significance of his consecration, we must understand the process by which olive oil is extracted from the fruit. After an olive tree has been cultivated and its fruit harvested, the olives are then crushed by weighted pressure, causing the oil to flow. Believers can learn a lesson from this process. Not until we are crushed will the oil flow. In other words, we will not produce a flow of blessing until we are broken open and crushed beneath God-ordained pressure. Our heavenly Father takes all of us through a process of being crushed so that His anointing will flow through us. There are no shortcuts to the genuine anointing flow. You may be able to receive a measure of revelation through impartation; still, it is the crushing that allows God's anointing—the anointing that produces results—to flow in abundance through an individual.

It was not a flippant thing for Samuel to anoint a man with oil to be the king of God's people. It was a serious matter. We see this as the prophet explained to God that he could not possibly anoint one of Jesse's sons, for it could cost him his life. *"And Samuel said, How can I go? if Saul hear it, he will kill me"* (1 Samuel 16:2). Oil was the visible, tangible representation of the Holy Spirit doing a *new thing.* When someone was anointed with oil, it was a declaration of the Holy Spirit empowering that person for a *new work.*

Both Saul and David were unexpectedly anointed to be king. Saul was searching for his father's donkeys prior to his anointing, while David was out in the field keeping his father's sheep. The Holy Spirit came on both men as they were anointed by the prophet Samuel. However, the similarities end there. When Samuel anointed Saul, he knew that Saul was coming because God had told him as much the day before.

> *Now the* Lord *had told Samuel in his ear a day before Saul came, saying, To morrow about this time I will send thee a man out of the land of Benjamin, and thou shalt anoint him to be captain over my people Israel, that he may save my people out of the hand of the Philistines: for I have looked upon my people, because their cry is come unto me.*
>
> (1 Samuel 9:15–16)

The Scriptures describe Saul as being *"higher than any other of the people from his shoulders and upward"* (1 Samuel 10:23). Saul looked the part. He was handsome, tall, and anointed by God. The Word proclaims that after he was anointed, God *"gave him another heart"* (1 Samuel 10:9). Samuel then threw a party celebrating Saul, the one whom God had chosen. He invited thirty of the most prestigious guests to celebrate the momentous occasion. David's anointing, on the other hand, was done in secret with no fanfare.

Saul and David were both anointed with the same oil and by the same prophet, but the circumstances and the containers used to anoint them could also not have been more different. I believe it was a deliberate prophetic act that God gave Samuel instructions to use the different vessels. Samuel used a *"vial of oil"* (1 Samuel 10:1) to anoint Saul. According to *Strong's Concordance*, the Hebrew word *pak*, translated *"vial,"* means a "vial," "flask," or "box." It was man-made. Remember, Israel had rejected God and no longer wanted to have a theocratic government. Instead, they wanted to be like the other nations. They cried out for a king. So, a man-made tool through which the oil flowed was appropriate. On the other hand, for David's anointing, God told Samuel to *"fill thine horn with oil"* (1 Samuel 16:1). The word *"horn"* was translated from the Hebrew word *qeren*, meaning "a horn of an ox, a goat or ram." It was a God-made container. It represents sacrifice and is used to convey power and strength.

When Samuel went to anoint David, God explicitly warned the great prophet not to be moved by his natural senses. He was announcing to Samuel that He was moving in a different direction, and it would not be as it had been before.

> *But the LORD said unto Samuel, Look not on his countenance, or on the height of his stature; because I have refused him: for the LORD seeth not as man seeth; for man looketh on the outward appearance, but the LORD looketh on the heart.*
>
> (1 Samuel 16:7)

Saul was impressive in stature. He looked the part of a king. But God did not want someone who pleased the flesh by only looking the part. God wanted a man after His own heart, and David was that man. (See Acts 13:22.) The Lord chose David, while the people chose Saul. God wanted one who had the right heart. In essence, God was saying, "The oil will flow over My vessel whom I have chosen. He is the least of his house, but he is My chosen one."

BE CAREFUL WHAT YOU WISH FOR

One may wonder why the Lord chose to anoint Saul at all. I've wondered that myself. God once said to me, "It was what the people wanted." Scripture certainly makes this clear. It records that the people said to Samuel,

> Behold, thou art old, and thy sons walk not in thy ways: now make us a king to judge us like all the nations. But the thing displeased Samuel, when they said, Give us a king to judge us. And Samuel prayed unto the LORD. And the LORD said unto Samuel, Hearken unto the voice of the people in all that they say unto thee: for they have not rejected thee, but they have rejected me, that I should not reign over them.
>
> (1 Samuel 8:5–7)

Sometimes, the Lord will give us what we want. We should be diligent in making sure our desires align with His Word and what He wants for us.

There have been times when my own desires have superseded God's desires for me—times when my intense longing nullified God's voice of warning, and the result was regret and frustration. This is precisely the trap that Israel had fallen prey to; they wanted what they wanted, and nothing the prophet had to say would dissuade them from pursuing it. Samuel warned them of the terrible consequences that would come because they decided to be like the other nations, but he could not persuade them to change their course of thinking.

> *And he said, This will be the manner of the king that shall reign over you: He will take your sons, and appoint them for himself, for his chariots, and to be his horsemen; and some shall run before his chariots. And he will appoint him captains over thousands, and captains over fifties; and will set them to ear his ground, and to reap his harvest, and to make his instruments of war, and instruments of his chariots. And he will take your daughters to be confectionaries, and to be cooks, and to be bakers. And he will take your fields, and your vineyards, and your oliveyards, even the best of them, and give them to his servants. And he will take the tenth of your seed, and of your vineyards, and give to his officers, and to his servants. And he will take your menservants, and your maidservants, and your goodliest young men, and your asses, and put them to his work. He will take the tenth of your sheep: and ye shall be his servants. And ye shall cry out in that day because of your king which ye shall have chosen you; and the LORD will not hear you in that day.* (1 Samuel 8:11–18)

Before you harshly judge Israel for rejecting God, ask yourself how many times you have rejected God's plans so that you could have your own way.

I remember, years ago, reading this text and crying over God's being rejected by His people, Israel. It truly broke my heart to read what God said to Samuel in 1 Samuel 8:7: "*They have not rejected you, but they have rejected Me*" (1 Samuel 8:7 NKJV). God spoke to me and said, "Andrew, how many times have you chosen what you wanted over My desire for you?" Wow! I was guilty of the same action I had tried and convicted the Israelites of. Have you ever settled for a Saul when God said, "I have better for you"? I know I have.

MOVE ON

Why are God's children, like the prophet Samuel, crying over the Sauls in their lives? The "Sauls" that I refer to are past things we had high hopes for—things we desired above all else but did not receive or did not produce the hoped-for results. God says to us, *"How long wilt thou mourn for Saul, seeing I have rejected him from reigning over Israel? fill thine horn with oil, and go"* (1 Samuel 16:1).

This is your time to move into the new. The past is over. It is time for you to birth the new! God is anointing you with fresh oil. Yesterday is over! Quit weeping over the past. God has rejected it. There is a David—something new—arising on the scene!

The Lord spoke to me, saying, "The Sauls are fading, and the Davids are rising." I truly believe that those whom the horn of God has anointed are now rising to the forefront. Those who have been appointed through the desires of man are fading into the background. There is a revival of purity that is taking place.

When the Lord first spoke this to me, I began to seek the Lord to find the differences between Saul and David. If you examine their lives, you see that both men were imperfect kings. Both men sinned and fell into compromise. The major difference between them was that David was always quick to repent and possessed a genuine holy fear of God. It wasn't about the position, for his kingship was a by-product of his relationship with God. Saul would rule most of his reign according to the flesh. He refused to submit to the Holy Spirit and instead leaned upon his fleshly reasoning. Again, we can see the symbolic difference in David's being a horn (God-made) and Saul's being a flask (man-made).

When you are God-made, as David was, God will spend more time taking you through the process before raising you up. After being anointed by Samuel, Saul was immediately thrust into the spotlight as the new king. David, after being anointed, was hidden.

He experienced life-changing battles. He faced twenty-one different attempts against his life from his former mentor. He had to run for his life, hiding in caves and living in a foreign country. Through it all, he learned to depend on God to protect him. His desperation drove him to further rely on God as his saving strength.

David penned the following words:

Thou preparest a table before me in the presence of mine enemies: thou anointest my head with oil; my cup runneth over.

(Psalm 23:5)

I declare over you today, "You will be anointed with fresh oil." When you inspect your own life, you may compare yourself to David without recognizing and confronting the "Saul" side of yourself. Most people are heroes in their own eyes, never realizing they also play the role of villain. The man-made flasks have to be crucified. I pray that you will allow the Holy Spirit to show you what needs to be conquered in your life so that you can fulfill God's plan and purpose for you.

Let's pray this prayer:

Holy Spirit, show me the areas in my life where my desires have been choking out God's desires. Create in me a clean heart and renew a right spirit within me. I ask You to help me be quick to repent, eager to complete my assignment on the earth, and, like David, enabled to fulfill everything that is in Your heart for me to do. In Jesus's name, amen.

9

STOPPING THE GATES OF HELL

My family loves going to Walt Disney World in Orlando, Florida. My wife, Brooke, worked for the Disney company in various positions for sixteen years before she moved back to our hometown of Chattanooga, Tennessee, to marry her very own Prince Charming. (Okay, I'm being a little facetious. But it's true that she left the Magic Kingdom to help me build the kingdom of God!)

While my wife continues to work alongside me in ministry, she was led to use her travel expertise to start a business that's thriving. Her specialty is helping families plan their own Disney vacations. This means she has to make frequent trips to Disney World, and our kids and I usually find a way to tag along.

Every time we arrive at Walt Disney World, we all go crazy with excitement. My children love seeing the pictures of Mickey and Minnie Mouse waving to us as we drive beneath the gates of the property. In fact, a childlike excitement is stirred within us all as memories flood our minds and we remember the fun times we've enjoyed together and anticipate the new fun we're about to share.

One particular trip to Disney stands out in my mind. We had driven from Chattanooga to Orlando, which generally takes around eight hours, but this trip was different. It rained from the moment we left our house all the way to Orlando. I am not talking about light showers here and there. It was a nonstop pounding of torrential rain. The constant downpour delayed our arrival. When we started our journey, our GPS gave us an estimated arrival time that did not take into account the slower-than-usual speed I would need to maintain because of the nonstop rain hindering my vision. There were times when it was raining so hard, I could scarcely see more than a few feet in front of me.

We prayed in the Holy Ghost almost the entire time. We finally reached the Orlando turnpike, and the rain increased. I was tired and stressed from driving in such conditions, but when we entered the gates and our children saw Mickey Mouse, suddenly, the mood in the car shifted from stress and frustration to pure excitement. Instead of whining about how tired they were, the kids giggled in anticipation of what was coming.

The Lord began to speak to me concerning gateways. He said very clearly to me, "Guard your gates. You are the gatekeeper of your anointing. The enemy is searching for an opening to your life." I began to dwell on what He had spoken to me.

GUARD THE GATES

Each of us has three major gateways that affect our soul: (1) the eye-gate (what we see), (2) the ear-gate (what we hear), and (3) the mouth-gate (what we speak). These gateways can serve as entry points for God's heavenly agenda to manifest—or as openings for the enemy to attempt to thwart God's plan for our lives. All three gateways are vital to the life of the believer, but I want to pay particular attention right now to the eye-gate.

You must protect what you see and where you allow your eyes to focus. David wrote:

> *I will lift up mine eyes unto the hills, from whence cometh my help. My help cometh from the* LORD, *which maketh heaven and earth.*   (Psalm 121:1–2)

It is crucial that we know where our help comes from and that we keep our gaze solely on God. One of the best examples of this truth is found in Matthew 14. In this account, Jesus's disciples were sailing in a boat when, at three in the morning, they saw a figure walking toward them on the water. Scripture tells us, *"They were terrified….But Jesus spoke to them at once. 'Don't be afraid,' he said. 'Take courage. I am here!'"* (Matthew 14:26–27 NLT). Watch what happens next.

> *Then Peter called to him, "Lord, if it's really you, tell me to come to you, walking on the water." "Yes, come," Jesus said. So Peter went over the side of the boat and walked on the water toward Jesus. But when he saw the strong wind and the waves, he was terrified and began to sink. "Save me, Lord!" he shouted. Jesus immediately reached out and grabbed him. "You have so little faith," Jesus said. "Why did you doubt me?"*
>
> (Matthew 14:28–31 NLT)

When Peter stepped out of the boat into the midst of a raging sea, he walked upon the water. It was only when he took his eyes off Jesus and looked at the boisterous winds and waves that he began to sink. This was an entrapment of the enemy. Satan had distracted Peter and directed his vision elsewhere. And he is after your vision, too. I have heard it said, "What you stare at longest becomes strongest in your life." It is true. If you stare at the contrary winds and the crashing waves, they will only become magnified in your life.

The enemy is a master of distraction. If he can cause you to turn your eyes away for even a moment, as he did to Peter, you also will begin to sink.

STEALING OUR VISION

The devil is in a desperate pursuit of our vision. He understands how powerful vision is in the life of the believer.

When there is no clear prophetic vision, people quickly wander astray. But when you follow the revelation of the Word, heaven's bliss fills your soul.   (Proverbs 29:18 TPT)

Did you catch that profound truth? Where there is no clear prophetic vision, people go astray. The King James Version says that they *"perish."* The Greek word for *"perish"* is *abad* and is defined as "wander away, lose oneself, by implication to perish, break, destroy, not escape, fail," and "lose." You must come to the following understanding: the enemy does not just want to hurt your feelings. He wants to destroy you. How can he accomplish this? By stealing your vision and directing your eye-gate to lead you into destruction.

Let's look now at an example of vision from the Old Testament. The people of Jabesh-Gilead were isolated and cut off from the other tribes of Israel after they failed to join their brethren in warring against the Benjamites to avenge the rape of the Levite priest's concubine by men of Benjamin. (See Judges 19.) Judges 21:6–14 records that four hundred virgins were taken alive from Jabesh-Gilead and given as wives to the Benjamites who survived after the civil war. Now, in 1 Samuel 11, the Ammonites had surrounded the people of Jabesh-Gilead, and it seemed as if their total defeat was inevitable. Indeed, they were already defeated in their minds. All the men of Jabesh-Gilead said to Nahash, the Ammonite, *"Make a covenant with us, and we will serve thee"* (1 Samuel 11:1). They were attempting to make a covenant with their enemy.

This is often how people try to remedy their opposition from the enemy. They inadvertently try to make a deal with the devil by telling him, for example, "I'll stop praying, attending church, and witnessing if you'll just leave me alone." The problem is that the enemy always has conditions for people to meet. This was undoubtedly true for Jabesh-Gilead.

> *And Nahash the Ammonite answered them, On this condition will I make a covenant with you, that I may thrust out all your right eyes, and lay it for a reproach upon all Israel.*
>
> (1 Samuel 11:2)

The Ammonites commanded that the men of Jabesh-Gilead thrust out their right eye to become a reproach upon Israel. The Greek word for *"reproach"* is *kher-paw*. It means "disgrace, rebuke," and "shame." Significantly, the demand from their enemy was for them to cast out their *"right"* eye. The Bible says that Jesus is seated at the right hand of the Father. (See, for example, Hebrews 12:2.) In other words, this act was to take away their power and authority, ensuring they would never revolt and would remain servants of the Ammonites forever.

When God's people lose their vision, it brings shame and disgrace. The elders of Jabesh-Gilead told the Ammonites to give them seven days to seek help from the new king of Israel, Saul. They sent messengers to the king to lay out their case. First Samuel 11:6–11 tells us that *"the Spirit of God came upon Saul when he heard those tidings, and his anger was kindled greatly"* (1 Samuel 11:6). Then Saul made a plan, and he told the men of Jabesh that by the time the sun got hot the following day, they would indeed have help. (See verse 9.)

Do you feel like the men of Jabesh, needing help but not seeing it on the horizon? I prophesy to you that *help is on its way*. Get ready for God's divine intervention. Do not allow the enemy to blur your vision by "thrusting out" your eye and disabling your authority. Remember that in the natural, Samson was blinded, but God bypassed his natural circumstances to give him a supernatural miracle to bring forth His plan for his life. He will do the same for you!

You are about to see God miraculously deliver you from the plot of the enemy. In fact, I heard the Spirit of the Lord say, "The haze of confusion is lifting, and the smog of desperation is leaving. Clarity will now be your new reality. Open your eyes. God is giving your fresh vision, and you have complete authority over your enemy!"

FRESH VISION

My grandmother spent the last few years of her life suffering from Alzheimer's disease. She deteriorated to the point that she was no longer was able to communicate with us and was confined to a hospital bed most of the time. It broke my heart to witness how this disease had ravaged her body and mind—the same disease that had plagued my grandmother's father, my great-grandfather. My grandmother would always say that she never wanted to end up bedridden like her father.

I often wondered why the Lord allowed her to linger on earth, suffering from Alzheimer's, rather than whisking her away to heaven to be with Him. One day out of the blue, I received a text message from my grandmother's nurse. It was a video of my grandmother, and she was praying in the Holy Ghost as she lay in her hospital bed. It was exactly how I remembered her praying when I was a young boy. I suddenly realized that God's Spirit had bypassed her natural mind and was making intercession through her. I am convinced that she was fulfilling God's purpose through her intercession. This incident drove home the fact that as long as there is breath in the believer's body, God has a plan for their life.

After being tormented by the demonic spirit that controlled Delilah, Samson wished for death. Hell's strategy had been put into motion in an attempt to overthrow the plan of God. If only Samson had recognized that he was in a spiritual battle and had taken authority over the evil powers, his life would have turned out as a very different story. The spirit of Delilah darkens your view until you can no longer recognize setups from hell. The enemy rejoices gleefully when his plot has enticed a child of God to close their eyes.

Samson closed his eyes to rest from the torment and spiritual warfare that encircled him. He slept in Delilah's lap. Yet torment was only a small taste of what was to come to him.

So the Philistines captured him and gouged out his eyes. They took him to Gaza, where he was bound with bronze chains and forced to grind grain in the prison. (Judges 16:21 NLT)

When Samson was taken captive, the Philistines gouged out his eyes. This was a common practice among ancient warriors. They would remove one eye or both to ensure that their rival could never again oppose them in battle. Usually, the right eye was taken, for it was used for looking at an enemy over the top of one's shield during combat.

The Philistines had gouged out Samson's eyes, shaved his head, and put him fetters. The great judge of Israel, the one who was called to deliver God's people, had been forced by his enemies to grind grain at the mill. Samson had fallen from the high state of exaltation to the low state of despair. He had become an object of scorn.

A revelatory nugget is contained in Judges 16:22: *"The hair of his head began to grow again."* I believe this statement is a picture of the restoration of Samson's relationship with God and the renewal of his vow as a Nazarite. His failure had cost him his natural sight, but now, through the eyes of the Spirit, his vision had never been clearer.

As I write these words, I hear the Lord beckoning to you, saying, "Get up from your brokenness. Quit allowing your failure to rob you of your destiny. There is restoration for you. I still have a plan and a purpose for your life. Stop looking with your natural eyes at the carnage your compromise has caused and start seeing with the eyes of the Spirit what I have declared over your life. I am not finished with you!"

YOU CAN BREAK FREE

One day Jesus asked His disciples two simple questions. The first one was, *"Whom do men say that I the Son of man am?"* (Matthew 16:13). They answered, *"Some say John the Baptist, some Elijah, and others Jeremiah or one of the prophets"* (Matthew 16:14 NKJV). Then came the second question, and Jesus made it personal: *"But whom say ye that I am?"* (Matthew 16:15). He asked them the second question to test their personal revelation. In essence, Jesus asked them, "You have heard what others think or say, but who am I to you?"

It is important that you have your own encounter with Jesus. It is not enough to live off your parents' relationship with Jesus or your favorite preacher's words about Jesus. He wants you to know Him. He desires for you to encounter Him and for the Holy Spirit to reveal Him to you. He does not want to be mere words on a page or just a historical figure to you. He wants to be more than just your Savior; He wants to be your Lord.

The disciple who answered Jesus correctly as to His identity was Peter:

> *And Simon Peter answered and said, Thou art the Christ, the Son of the living God. And Jesus answered and said unto him, Blessed art thou, Simon Barjona: for flesh and blood hath not*

revealed it unto thee, but my Father which is in heaven. And I say also unto thee, That thou art Peter, and upon this rock I will build my church; and the gates of hell shall not prevail against it. And I will give unto thee the keys of the kingdom of heaven: and whatsoever thou shalt bind on earth shall be bound in heaven: and whatsoever thou shalt loose on earth shall be loosed in heaven. (Matthew 16:16–19)

This portion of Scripture has been misinterpreted by many Christians. Contrary to what countless people may insist, Peter is *not* the rock upon which the church is built. It is upon the revelation that Jesus is the Son of God that the church is built. The name Peter is translated from the Greek word *petros*, which means "fragment of a rock." Peter was one of the builders, but Christ alone is the foundation.

For no one can lay a foundation other than the one which is [already] laid, which is Jesus Christ.
(1 Corinthians 3:11 AMP)

The Greek word translated *"church"* in Matthew 16:18 is *ekklesia*, meaning "legislative assembly" or "selected ones." Interestingly, it is not a religious term at all, but rather a political and governmental term used many times in classical Greek for a group of people who have been summoned and gathered to govern the affairs of a city. For Jesus to have used this term means He was giving the keys of governmental authority in His kingdom to the church.

Jesus ordained His church to be a legislative assembly. He gave to all believers—yourself included—the authority to govern the earth. Yet the church has often shirked her responsibility and allowed the enemy to rule instead. This abdication is a symptom of having come under the influence of the spirit of Delilah. Samson had been chosen by God to defeat the Philistines and bring deliverance to Israel, but by breaking his vows to God, he forfeited his authority. Today, we see that very forfeiture being replayed again and again. If ever God has sounded the alarm for the church to awaken, He's doing it now!

Jesus said that when the church arises in its God-given authority, "*the gates of hell shall not prevail against it*" (Matthew 16:18). Gates were of great significance for cities in the ancient world. They were the entrance points, as well as the places where business transactions would occur. They served as gathering locations for social, commercial, and judicial activities. The city gates are also where leaders and officials would meet, including judges, kings, and prophets. For example, Ahab and Jehoshaphat sat at the gate: "*And the king of Israel and Jehoshaphat the king of Judah sat each on his throne, having put on their robes, in a void place in the entrance of the gate of Samaria; and all the prophets prophesied before them*" (1 Kings 22:10).

Jesus was saying that the meeting place of hell's demonic forces—the place where they strategize and plan attacks against His church—would not prevail against the church. Satan's plans will not prevail against you. You are breaking free from the Delilah spirit's attacks against you and your family.

No weapon that is formed against thee shall prosper; and every tongue that shall rise against thee in judgment thou shalt condemn. This is the heritage of the servants of the Lord, *and their righteousness is of me, saith the* Lord. (Isaiah 54:17)

10

HOW TO BREAK DELILAH'S CHOKEHOLD

While I was writing this book, the enemy repeatedly tried to hinder me from completing the project. Out of nowhere, I found myself feeling depleted, discouraged, and downcast. There was no reason in the natural that I should have been feeling that way. My family was doing great, our church was growing, new doors were opening, and we had experienced some of the most powerful services in the history of our ministry. None of what I was feeling made any sense.

I reached out to many of my ministry friends who have written books about warfare, prayer, and revival to inquire if they had faced an unusual amount of conflict while writing about these topics. They all, without exception, confirmed they had.

So I went to my prayer room and began to pray, saying, "Lord, I don't understand why I'm feeling this way. There is no reason in the natural that I should be feeling so low. I know that this must be a supernatural attack." The Lord spoke to me, "It is the spirit of

Delilah. It is pressing you because you are exposing it. Rise up and take authority over it."

The enemy was working behind the scenes. The Delilah spirit was attempting to catch me in its crosshairs. The devil does not want his battle plans exposed, and he does not want you to have the guidebook for walking in complete victory.

When the spirit of Delilah has laid siege against you, you stop prioritizing God's presence. Entertainment and other distractions begin to occupy your thoughts. In many cases, an overwhelming feeling of tiredness will envelop you, regardless of the amount or quality of sleep you have been getting.

Fortunately, the first step to victory is recognizing that you are under assault.

RECOGNIZING THE ATTACK

After the Lord confirmed that I was being pressed by the spirit of Delilah, I jumped to my feet and began to bind its power by speaking aloud. I said, "Devil, I know you are trying to make me lay my head in your lap, and that you are pressing me in in the hopes of getting me exasperated, but it's not going to work. I am awake, and I refuse to allow this attack to continue for one more minute. I declare that I live in revival. I walk in the Spirit, and I will not fulfill the lusts of the flesh. I am filled with Holy Ghost boldness. The same Spirit that raised Christ from the dead lives in me, and He has quickened me. You have no authority, and you have to break now, in Jesus's name!" Immediately, the haze lifted, and my vision became clear. This experience charged me even more to finish this book and get it into your hands because now is your time to live free.

Kenneth Hagin was quoted as saying that knowledge is half the battle won, and he was right. Discernment is one of the keys to winning this battle. We tend to look at Samson and think,

"How could he not have known that Delilah was setting him up for betrayal?" Perhaps we could excuse him for being unaware the first time she attempted to manipulate him to reveal the secret to his supernatural strength to her. But after she followed through and acted upon his fabricated answers to her interrogation, why did he allow her to further question him? How could he have been that blind?

Discernment is a gift from God. It is the ability to differentiate between truth and lies. It sees the spirit behind words, actions, and deeds. *"But strong meat belongeth to them that are of full age, even those who by reason of use have their senses exercised to discern both good and evil"* (Hebrews 5:14). This is a gift that every believer should desire and cultivate in their life. It will save you from a lot of mistakes and heartache.

HEEDING THE RED FLAGS

I would like to share a story that I touched on in an earlier chapter, from a different angle. There was a time in my ministry when a particular couple came into our church with such zeal and excitement about our church's vision. I was thrilled by their exceptional skills and talent. My wife and I developed a friendship with this couple, as well as a close ministerial relationship. They attended every service and were always willing to help in whatever areas they were needed. We relied on them quite a bit.

Eventually, though, I started noticing certain actions and behaviors that concerned me. There were a few fleeting comments they had made about their previous leaders that gave me pause, but I quickly excused them, telling myself I was probably misinterpreting the situation. I really didn't want to hear any cautions concerning this couple. I allowed my enthusiasm to silence the alarm bells that should have been blaring a loud, clear warning.

After a little while, I noticed that this couple started coming late or not at all for corporate prayer. I wondered if they were mad or offended at me. From personal experience, I know you can't pray with someone and be angry with them at the same time. If I've had a disagreement with someone, or if someone has hurt me, the offense usually lifts as I pray for that person. The enemy knows how the power of agreement works against him, and he will do everything he can to stir strife and division to keep believers from warring together against him.

It became increasingly evident that something was brewing behind the scenes with this couple. Several others on my leadership team came to me and expressed concern over the habit of this couple to remain in the church foyer or nursery whenever I ministered. Finally, I spoke with this couple and asked them if everything was okay. They assured me that everything was fine. They said they had been staying in the foyer because their child refused to go to the nursery and only wanted them. Having young children of my own, I fully understood that sometimes it is only the parent that can comfort their child. I accepted their explanation.

But when the same thing happened week after week, I found it hard to believe that their child, who had been going into the same class with the same teacher since birth, suddenly no longer wanted to go. I stopped making excuses for the parents. Something was up.

It wasn't long after I had talked with the couple that I learned they had approached several families in the church to criticize our leadership and plant seeds of the idea that they would be better leaders. This divisive behavior, prompted by the betraying spirit of Delilah, caused a split in our church split and did major damage to the kingdom of God. This couple ultimately started their own church down the road from us, hurting a lot of families in the process.

Sometimes we dismiss red flags of warning because we don't want to face the truth, particularly if we have had invested in someone and given them roles of responsibility and influence, as I had done with this couple in our church body. Let me exhort you: whenever there is a question mark in your spirit about a person, take it to the Lord in prayer and ask Him to reveal to you the reason for it.

In the situation I have just described, I completely ignored God's warning because I wanted so badly to believe that this couple would never intentionally hurt the church or me. I imagine this was how Samson felt. He wanted to believe Delilah was who she portrayed herself to be. He loved Delilah. (See Judges 16:4.) He chose to believe that she loved him. He envisioned their future together. He longed for a place of safety where he would find rest. He was carrying the weight of a nation on his shoulders. He thought Delilah was more than a beautiful woman. He believed she was the one. He imagined that they would share more than just a romantic tryst. The mighty judge of Israel, who possessed supernatural strength and defeated entire armies, opened his heart to Delilah. He believed that she would receive and reciprocate his love. He was wrong about her, just as I was wrong about that couple, who had clearly allowed the spirit of Delilah to overtake them.

David faced similar trouble and heartache from his son Absalom. The story of Absalom's betrayal can be found in the book of 2 Samuel, and the following is an excerpt.

[Absalom] *got up early every morning and went out to the gate of the city. When people brought a case to the king for judgment, Absalom would ask where in Israel they were from, and they would tell him their tribe. Then Absalom would say, "You've really got a strong case here! It's too bad the king doesn't have anyone to hear it. I wish I were the judge. Then everyone could bring their cases to me for judgment, and I would give them justice!" When people tried to bow before him, Absalom wouldn't let them. Instead, he took them by the hand and kissed them. Absalom did this with everyone who came to the king for judgment, and so he stole the hearts of all the people of Israel.* (2 Samuel 15:2–6 NLT)

Observe how Absalom worked against his father, David. He methodically encountered the people, one by one, before they reached the king for judgment. He subtly criticized David's leadership, basically saying to the people, "The king doesn't have time for you," followed by, "*I wish I were the judge. Then everyone could bring their cases to me, and I would give them justice!*" In other words, he was saying, "I would be a better leader than my father. I would solve all your problems." And when the people would try to bow before him, Absalom would put on a show of false humility, thereby stealing their hearts.

I have seen this exact scenario play out time and time again in churches, businesses, ministries, marriages, and other entities. It starts with an individual or a group that desires what another possesses. Envy is one of Satan's most brutal weapons. It stops at nothing to gain the very thing it desires for itself, leaving destruction in its wake.

BIRTHED FROM THE FLESH

Before I married Brooke, I dated another girl, even though I knew she was not the one God had for me. One night, I was walking the floor, praying and pleading my cause to the Lord. I asked Him to please bless our relationship. I heard God's voice so clearly. He said, "I did not birth it, and I will not bless it." I knew right then that this relationship was not God's plan for me. As much as it hurt me to end our relationship, I did not want to wear myself out trying to maintain something my flesh had birthed. I have heard it said, and I find it to be true: "What you birth in the flesh, you must maintain in the flesh. What is born of the spirit will be maintained by the Spirit." Your flesh "babies" will wear you out. They will rob you of your resources, your emotions, and, most of all, your time with God.

God will not bless anything that has been possessed through means that are illegal in the spirit. What God did not birth, He will not bless. What is born of the flesh is of the flesh (see John 3:6), meaning you cannot birth things through the flesh and then expect God to bless them.

Abraham is an excellent example of someone who birthed something of the flesh—literally—and then asked God to bless it. Back when he was still called Abram, he had been given a promise from God that he would become a great nation (see Genesis 12:2–3), but it had not yet come to pass. Scripture tells us that, rather than waiting on and trusting God's timing, Abram and his wife, Sarai, chose to take matters into their own hands.

> *Now Sarai, Abram's wife, had not been able to bear children for him. But she had an Egyptian servant named Hagar. So Sarai said to Abram, "The LORD has prevented me from having children. Go and sleep with my servant. Perhaps I can have children through her." And Abram agreed with Sarai's proposal. So Sarai, Abram's wife, took Hagar the Egyptian servant and gave her to Abram as a wife. (This happened ten years after Abram had settled in the land of Canaan.) So Abram had sexual relations with Hagar, and she became pregnant.* (Genesis 16:1–4 NLT)

Satan knows that if he can delay the fulfillment of God's promises long enough, it will cause many believers to give up and take matters into their own hands. Delay and disappointment will drive believers to operate in their flesh, seeking to bring God's promises to fruition in their own power.

Abram didn't give much resistance to Sarai's plan of helping God out. I have learned that God does not need our help to fulfill His Word. He requires our obedience. Sarai's plan of the flesh was indeed successful. Hagar conceived and birthed a son named Ishmael, but Ishmael was a counterfeit of the promised child and eventually began to mock Isaac, who was the true child of promise later born to Abraham and Sarah in their old age.

Now [as time went on] Sarah saw [Ishmael] the son of Hagar the Egyptian, whom she had borne to Abraham, mocking [Isaac]. (Genesis 21:9 AMP)

Just like Ishmael mocked Isaac, so too will your work of the flesh mock your true promise.

Samson had birthed his relationship with Delilah by the flesh, and so, like everything that is birthed by the flesh, it left him depleted and vulnerable. He was unable to recognize that he was in a spiritual battle. Satan had ensnared him to birth that which God had forbidden. The demonic spirit that operated through Delilah had trapped Samson exactly where it wanted him. He had become powerless against its relentless oppression, even to the point of wishing for death. (See Judges 16:16.)

It was precisely at the moment when Samson's defenses were down, and he was completely broken, that the evil one struck him. He was betrayed by the woman he loved, and, even more devastating than that, Samson had betrayed the One who really loved him. The hair on his head was a sign of his devotion to God, and he had sacrificed it to the spirit of Delilah.

While writing this, I could not help but imagine how Samson must have felt when his love betrayed him. In the very next moment, my thoughts turned to how God must have felt when Samson betrayed Him. This time, the disloyalty wasn't his love divulging the answer to a riddle, which he could readily avenge by tying a torch between the tails of two foxes and sending them forth to burn the Philistines' crops. No, this time, Samson gambled his relationship with God against his love for Delilah and lost.

BREAKING OUT OF DELILAH'S CLUTCHES

The spirit of Delilah threatens to ensnare us by causing us to overlook red flags and compelling us to carry out plans of the flesh rather than trusting God to fulfill His promises to us. It threatens to lead us on a path of destruction that unravels our relationship with God. The good news is, we are not helpless before the spirit of Delilah. There is hope and help for overcoming this wily demon.

Before we can begin breaking away from the spirit of Delilah, as I've said before, we must identify that we are under attack. Then, we must push back against the assault and determinedly submit to God and resist the enemy.

So submit to [the authority of] God. Resist the devil [stand firm against him] and he will flee from you. (James 4:7 AMP)

It is vital that we recognize the enemy against whom we are fighting. In Ephesians 16, the apostle Paul outlines the militant positions of Satan's kingdom. *The Passion Translation* renders this text as follows:

Your hand-to-hand combat is not with human beings, but with the highest principalities and authorities operating in rebellion under the heavenly realms. For they are a powerful class of demon-gods and evil spirits that hold this dark world in bondage. (Ephesians 6:12 TPT)

The first group listed is a group of spirits called principalities. The word *"principalities"* was translated from the Greek word *ar-khay* and is defined as "chief (in various applications of order, time, place, or rank):—beginning, (at the) first." Principalities are chief in rank, and the Greek word denotes that they were "at the first." They were thought to be the angels who were cast out of heaven with Lucifer.

Next on Paul's list are *"powers."* The word *"powers"* is translated from the Greek word *exousía* and is defined as "delegated influence, authority, jurisdiction, liberty, power, right" and "strength."

Paul goes on to rank two other evil groups described just below *"principalities"* and *"powers"*: *"rulers of the darkness of this world"* and *"spiritual wicked in high places."* The word *"rulers"* is a combination of two Greek words: *kósmos*, meaning "orderly arrangement," and *kratéō*, meaning "to use strength." Here Paul is referring to spirits that have ordered strength. They grip and take siege. *"Spiritual wickedness in high places"* can be defined as "depravity, malice, evil purposes and desires."

Those evil agents listed by Paul were given delegated jurisdiction to perform a plethora of attacks. They are given the liberty to execute evil strikes against humanity. Rick Renner explains,

> [T]he compounded word kosmokrateros depicts raw power that has been harnessed and put into some kind of order.
>
> This word kosmokrateros was at times used to picture military training camps where young men were assembled, trained, and turned into a mighty army. These young men were like raw power when they first arrived in the training camp. However, as the military training progressed and the new recruits were taught discipline and order, all that raw manpower was converted into an organized, disciplined army. This is the word Paul now uses in his description of Satan's kingdom.[11]

---

11. Rick Renner, "The Rank and File of Satan's Kingdom," Renner.org, https://renner.org/article/the-rank-and-file-of-satans-kingdom/.

As intimidating as this enemy may sound, remember that God has given you spiritual armor—not fleshly weapons—to combat the enemy and engage with him.

Put on God's complete set of armor provided for us, so that you will be protected as you fight against the evil strategies of the accuser!...Wear all the armor that God provides so you're protected as you confront the slanderer, for you are destined for all things and will rise victorious. Put on truth as a belt to strengthen you to stand in triumph. Put on holiness as the protective armor that covers your heart. Stand on your feet alert, then you'll always be ready to share the blessings of peace. In every battle, take faith as your wrap-around shield, for it is able to extinguish the blazing arrows coming at you from the evil one! Embrace the power of salvation's full deliverance, like a helmet to protect your thoughts from lies. And take the mighty razor-sharp Spirit-sword of the spoken word of God.
(Ephesians 6:11, 13–17 TPT)

God calls us to depend on Him in the power of His might, realizing that we are no match for the devil in our own strength. *"Finally, my brethren, be strong in the Lord, and in the power of his might"* (Ephesians 6:10). The Lord will not fail you. He will not allow you to be tempted above what you are able. He's already made a way of escape for you. *"There hath no temptation taken you but such as is common to man: but God is faithful, who will not suffer you to be tempted above that ye are able; but will with the temptation also make a way to escape, that ye may be able to bear it"* (1 Corinthians 10:13).

11

IT'S TIME FOR YOUR COMEBACK

And she made him sleep upon her knees; and she called for a man, and she caused him to shave off the seven locks of his head; and she began to afflict him, and his strength went from him. And she said, The Philistines be upon thee, Samson. And he awoke out of his sleep, and said, I will go out as at other times before, and shake myself. And he wist not that the LORD was departed from him. (Judges 16:19–20)

Samson had endured the most grievous spiritual, mental, and emotional attack of his life. He was well acquainted with physical battles, but he was not spiritually prepared to take on the demonic spirit that controlled Delilah. Unfortunately, before facing off against this demonic force, Samson was already spiritually bankrupt. As I have described in previous chapters, his compromise had put him in free fall without anything to catch him. He was a man overboard, floundering in a sea of sin and compromise.

Samson had no one to speak the truth to him in love. Although Samson's parents did question his desire to marry a Philistine bride, they let it go without much confrontation. We all need someone to speak the truth to us, especially if we are leaders. If only one of Samson's brethren had said to him, "Samson, I am very concerned about your compromised lifestyle. You are not living according to the Word of God."

Having strong spiritual mothers and fathers is crucial to your spiritual success. When I first began preaching, I had partnered with a church so that I could host meetings in their building. Everything went smoothly for the first couple of months. We saw souls saved and people healed and delivered. However, after the initial success, the ministry leaders called me into their office to discuss what they did not like about the services. They had a whole list of items they wanted to go over with me. They started the conversation by communicating how excited they were about the way God had been moving in our midst. But as they transitioned into airing their list of fifty critiques, I felt my confidence begin to wane. I have always tried to remain open to the influence and teachings of godly mentors. This feedback, however, was different. It seemed that with every point these leaders shared, my spirit became more downcast. There was a heaviness in the room. When one of them said, "You sweat too much. You need to control that," I heard the voice of the Holy Spirit say to me, "Andrew, their motive is not to help you to become more effective in communicating the gospel. They have given themselves over to a critical spirit, and it's attacking your anointing. Shake the dust off your feet and move forward." I did just that, and I'm so thankful I did. Samson desperately needed a voice to speak into his life, but the voice needed to be one that spoke the truth in love, as Ephesians 4:15 instructs us to do.

THE DESTROYER DESTROYED

After Samson was pressed night and day by his demonic foe and tormented by Delilah's manipulating words, he became so completely drained and depleted that he told her the secret to his strength. As soon as she learned the answer, Delilah moved against God's champion. She didn't even think twice. She made him sleep upon her knees. This is the Delilah spirit's habitual way of operating against God's people—by luring and enticing, controlling and manipulating. This spirit hounds and torments its prey, then it seeks to lull its target to sleep so that it can strike to destroy. Delilah called for a man to come and shave locks of Samson's hair while he slept in her lap. After the betrayal, it says that *"she began to afflict him"* (Judges 16:19). The word *"afflict,"* translated from the Hebrew word *anah*, means "browbeat, hurt" and "defile."

> *And she said, The Philistines be upon thee, Samson. And he awoke out of his sleep, and said, I will go out as at other times before, and shake myself. And he wist not that the LORD was departed from him.* (Judges 16:20)

To me, one of the saddest parts of the story is that Samson had taken his sin one step too far. He had given way to the spirit of Delilah, and the Lord had departed from him. He thought he could go out as he had always done before, and the Spirit of God would anoint him. Yet he had lost what mattered most: his relationship with God.

> *But the Philistines took him, and put out his eyes, and brought him down to Gaza, and bound him with fetters of brass; and he did grind in the prison house.* (Judges 16:21)

The Philistines took God's deliverer and gouged out his eyes. As I mentioned earlier, this type of torture was commonly done to ensure the defeated warrior would never again attain greatness in battle. I can only imagine what Samson must have been thinking as they put out his eyes. He must have replayed in his mind all the times that God supernaturally moved on him to experience great victories in which he defeated the very men who now tormented him. The shame of having failed God must have seemed unbearable, coupled with the hopelessness of thinking he would never accomplish the full purpose God had ordained for his life.

The Philistines bound him with bronze chains and made him grind grain in the prison house—a job that was usually reserved for enslaved women. They made Samson do the work of female slaves to further humiliate him and mock Israel. Samson could not have been reduced any lower. There was nothing they could have done to degrade him more than they did.

The Philistines rejoiced and offered sacrifices to their god, Dagon, for their victory over Samson, whom they called *"the destroyer of our country"* (Judges 16:24). In giving him this title, they recognized that Samson's purpose in life was to destroy their country and deliver the people of Israel. They may not have recognized God as the designer of Samson's purpose, but Satan and his demonic hordes certainly did. And Satan always seeks to oppose God's plans for His children. That is precisely why he has assigned his demons to attack and attempt to overwhelm you, in an effort to render you powerless and defeated.

REBOUND

Judges 16:22 tells us, *"The hair of his head began to grow again after he was shaven"* (Judges 16:22). Remember, the hair of Samson's head represented his separation and devotion unto God. This is where we begin to see God's champion rebound from the attack of the Delilah spirit. It started with his relationship with God. It was not about his anointing. It wasn't about returning as the judge of Israel. It was about being restored as a man of God. God is rich in mercy.

It is of the LORD's mercies that we are not consumed, because
his compassions fail not. They are new every morning: great is
thy faithfulness.   (Lamentations 3:22–23)

How can you rebound after being attacked by the spirit of
Delilah? The secret is found in Lamentations 3:22–23: "*The*
LORD's mercies...his compassions...his faithfulness." You can recover
from the Delilah spirit's attacks by seeking God. That may sound
overly simplistic, but God desires for you to win. He sent His Son,
Jesus, to redeem you. He does not want Satan to triumph. No!
You are called to rule and reign. He has given to you power over
the enemy.

Samson began to seek God while he was weak, enslaved, and
grinding in the mill. As the hair upon his head began to grow,
so did his devotion to God. God has set you up for a comeback,
as well. The enemy's attacks may have sidelined you for a season,
but the war isn't over. The enemy would love to convince you that
there's no way out of your failures and flaws, but, remember, he is a
liar and the father of lies. (See John 8:44.) God has made a way of
escape for you! He goes before you and makes the crooked places
straight.

I will go before thee, and make the crooked places straight: I
will break in pieces the gates of brass, and cut in sunder the
bars of iron.   (Isaiah 45:2)

You must live a lifestyle of pursuing God at all times, especially when the enemy has attacked you. The strength to rebound
from the devil's assaults is found only in a solid relationship with
God. You cannot do it on your own or by natural means. You are
fighting an invisible enemy in an invisible war, and only God can
empower you to triumph over your adversary. Your weapons only
become "*mighty through God*":

For the weapons of our warfare are not carnal, but mighty through God to the pulling down of strongholds.

(2 Corinthians 10:4)

COMEBACK

When Samson desperately tried to shake off Delilah's final attack, as he had done before, he discovered that the Lord had left him. Sleeping in the lap of Delilah rather than resisting her assault had cost him everything. The good news, though, is that it did not end there. While Samson was locked in prison and bound by the shame of his failure, he remembered his covenant with God. The hair on his head began to grow again as Samson returned to his first love. The enemy wanted him bound by fetters to bring about his ultimate demise, but God allowed him to be imprisoned to bring about his restoration and his greatest victory yet.

Judges 16:25 tells us that Samson had become the entertainment, the show, and the object of ridicule for the enemies of God.

And it came to pass, when their hearts were merry, that they said, Call for Samson, that he may make us sport. And they called for Samson out of the prison house; and he made them sport: and they set him between the pillars.   (Judges 16:25)

The very one who had killed thirty men the first time he had fought against the Philistines (see Judges 14:19), slaughtered *"many"* on the next occasion (see Judges 15:8), and killed one thousand the last time he had fought against them (see Judges 15:16) had now become their laughingstock. To put this in proper context, the Philistines, after they had brought Samson to his knees, eyed this Hebrew warrior not as the former killing machine he had been, who had previously won victory after victory for Israel against them, but as their great source of entertainment, even likened to the gladiators who made sport in the arenas for the Romans in the early-church days.

Judges 16:27 tells us, *"All the lords of the Philistines were there"*— about three thousand people—*"that beheld while Samson made sport."* Samson leaned against the pillars in the temple, and then he called on the Lord, pleading, *"Remember me"* (Judges 16:28). I love that he cried out for God to remember him. If you feel forgotten, you, too, can cry out for God to remember you.

Genesis 8:1, one of my favorite passages in Scripture, helps us understand what *"remember"* means in this context:

> *And God remembered Noah, and every living thing, and all the cattle that was with him in the ark: and God made a wind to pass over the earth, and the waters assuaged.*
> (Genesis 8:1)

That word *"remembered"* does not imply that God had forgotten Noah and his family were in the ark. No, it conveys that God moved for Noah through His covenant promise. Likewise, here in the book of Judges, Samson was not praying, "Remember that I am here, God." No, he was asking God to move for him. Specifically, he asked God, *"Strengthen me, I pray thee, only this once, O God, that I may be at once avenged of the Philistines for my two eyes"* (Judges 16:28).

God granted Samson his request.

> *And Samson said, Let me die with the Philistines. And he bowed himself with all his might; and the house fell upon the lords, and upon all the people that were therein. So the dead which he slew at his death were more than they which he slew in his life.*
> (Judges 16:30)

Samson killed more Philistines in his death than he had in his life. This is a picture of God granting someone a comeback after the enemy's attack. Indeed, Samson's story is included in what is called the "hall of faith" recorded in Hebrews 11. It further proves Samson's restoration and the fulfillment of God's plan for his life.

> *And what more could I say to convince you? For there is not enough time to tell you of the faith of Gideon, Barak, Samson, Jephthah, David, Samuel, and the prophets. Through faith's power they conquered kingdoms and established true justice. Their faith fastened onto their promises and pulled them into reality! It was faith that shut the mouth of lions, put out the power of raging fire, and caused many to escape certain death by the sword. Although weak, their faith imparted power to make them strong! Faith sparked courage within them and they became mighty warriors in battle, pulling armies from another realm into battle array.*   (Hebrews 11:32–34 TPT)

DECLARATIONS, SCRIPTURES, AND PRAYERS TO BREAK THE SPIRIT OF DELILAH

1. DECLARATION

I break the spirit of Delilah over my life, thoughts, and assignment. I am God's champion and have been called for such a time as this. I will fulfill all that He has purposed for me. I bind every demonic spirit sent to thwart God's plan and cause me to be lethargic.

SCRIPTURE

I assure you and most solemnly say to you, whatever you bind [forbid, declare to be improper and unlawful] on earth shall have [already] been bound in heaven, and whatever you loose [permit, declare lawful] on earth shall have [already] been loosed in heaven. (Matthew 18:18 AMP)

PRAYER

I bind every demonic power that is sent to steal, kill, and destroy. In the name of Jesus, you must go now and never return. I loose the flow of God's power and revelation in my life. Thank You, Lord, for moving in me, for me, and through me. I pray this in Jesus's name. Amen.

2. DECLARATION

I live awakened to the Spirit of God. My gates (eyes, ears, and mouth) are open for God to speak to me and through me, and to use me to speak a word in due season to others.

SCRIPTURE

The Lord GOD has given Me the tongue of the learned, that I should know how to speak a word in season to him who is weary. He awakens Me morning by morning, He awakens My ear to hear as the learned. (Isaiah 50:4 NKJV)

PRAYER

Lord, I thank You for awakening my ear to hear Your voice. I thank You for putting a word in my mouth to speak to the right person at just the right time. My steps are ordered by You. In the name of Jesus, I pray. Amen.

3. DECLARATION

I am victorious in every battle. I am an overcomer because I walk in the authority of Jesus.

SCRIPTURE

Listen carefully: I have given you authority [that you now possess] to tread on serpents and scorpions, and [the ability to exercise authority] over all the power of the enemy (Satan); and nothing will [in any way] harm you. (Luke 10:19 AMP)

PRAYER

Lord, thank You that I have authority over all the powers of the enemy. He cannot overtake, harm, or defeat me. You have given me the complete victory through the price that Jesus paid on the cross. In Jesus's name, amen.

4. DECLARATION

I walk in boldness and power. My prayers cause hell to tremble and heaven to answer. God hears and answers when I call to Him.

SCRIPTURE

This is the [remarkable degree of] confidence which we [as believers are entitled to] have before Him: that if we ask anything according to His will, [that is, consistent with His plan and purpose] He hears us. And if we know [for a fact, as indeed we do] that He hears and listens to us in whatever we ask, we [also] know [with settled and absolute knowledge] that we have [granted to us] the requests which we have asked from Him. (1 John 5:14–15 AMP)

PRAYER

Lord, I ask You to bless me with increase by giving me boldness in my prayer life. Help me to pray with authority and power. I thank You that, according to Your Word, when I pray, mountains move, the sick are healed, and devils are cast out. Anoint me with a fresh mantle of intercession. In Jesus's name, amen.

5. DECLARATION

I am equipped for battle and armed for war. I will not be afraid, and I will not quit. God is on my side. I am a giant-slayer.

SCRIPTURE

Praise the LORD, who is my rock. He trains my hands for war and gives my fingers skill for battle. He is my loving ally and my fortress, my tower of safety, my rescuer. He is my shield, and I take refuge in him. He makes the nations submit to me. (Psalm 144:1–2 NLT)

PRAYER

Father, I thank You that You have trained me for this war and equipped me for every battle. You have already defeated my enemy and secured my victory. I will follow Your leading and stay in the safety of Your shadow. In Jesus's name, amen.

6. DECLARATION

I am established in truth. I prosper in every area of my life (spiritually, physically, mentally, financially, and relationally).

SCRIPTURE

> So they rose early in the morning and went out into the Wilderness of Tekoa; and as they went out, Jehoshaphat stood and said, "Hear me, O Judah and you inhabitants of Jerusalem: Believe in the LORD your God, and you shall be established; believe His prophets, and you shall prosper."
>
> (2 Chronicles 20:20 NKJV)

PRAYER

God, I believe in You! Thank You for establishing me on a firm foundation. I believe Your prophets and Your Word. Thank You that I prosper. I ask You to make me whole in every area of my life. You give me good success in everything that I do. Amen.

7. DECLARATION

What God has ordained for my destiny will be established and completed. No assignment from hell can stop what God has decreed!

SCRIPTURE

I know that you can do all things, and that no purpose of yours can be thwarted. (Job 42:2 ESV)

PRAYER

Father, I thank You that I was created for Your purpose, and every word that You have spoken over my life will come to pass. You are faithful, and Your promises are true. In Your Son Jesus's name I pray, amen.

8. DECLARATION

I have been authorized to do the works of Jesus. I am equipped, empowered, and sent, and I will accomplish my assignment on the earth.

SCRIPTURE

> *Then Jesus said to them again, "Peace to you; as the Father has sent Me, I also send you [as My representatives]."*
>
> (John 20:21 AMP)

PRAYER

Lord, I thank You for choosing me to be Your representative on the earth. Help me be sensitive to the leading of the Holy Spirit and to walk in obedience to fulfill Your mandate. Amen.

9. DECLARATION

I can identify and discern setups from the enemy. I will neither compromise my assignment nor jeopardize my anointing. I resist the enemy, and he must flee. I live in complete freedom.

SCRIPTURE

So submit to [the authority of] God. Resist the devil [stand firm against him] and he will flee from you. (James 4:7 AMP)

PRAYER

Lord, I submit my will to Your authority. I ask You to give me strength to resist every temptation the enemy sends against me. Amen.

10. DECLARATION

I am awakened, revived, and on fire for God. I will not lay my head in Delilah's lap. I break off lethargy, apathy, and indifference over my life. I am awake and clearheaded.

SCRIPTURE

So then let us not sleep [in spiritual indifference] as the rest [of the world does], but let us keep wide awake [alert and cautious] and let us be sober [self-controlled, calm, and wise.]

(1 Thessalonians 5:6 AMP)

PRAYER

Heavenly Father, I ask You to help me stay awake and passionate about You and Your presence. I ask that You would breathe life into what seem like dead promises. Let me burn with hunger for You. In Jesus's name, amen.

11. DECLARATION

I am more than a conqueror through Christ Jesus. I not only conquer the enemy's plots in my life, but I am empowered to strengthen others to overcome his entrapments.

SCRIPTURE

Yet even in the midst of all these things, we triumph over them all, for God has made us to be more than conquerors, and his demonstrated love is our glorious victory over everything!

(Romans 8:37 TPT)

PRAYER

Heavenly Father, I thank You that You sent Your Son to show Your love for me. You have made me to be more than a conqueror. Send me to the ones whom You have ordained for me to strengthen. Open the door for me to speak a word to the weary. Amen.

12. DECLARATION

I walk in the favor of God. He has ordered my steps and ordained my path. I will not turn to the right or the left. I declare that I will walk in synchronization with the Holy Spirit.

SCRIPTURE

> *The steps of a [good and righteous] man are directed and established by the LORD, and He delights in his way [and blesses his path].* (Psalm 37:23 AMP)

PRAYER

> Thank You, Lord, for ordering my steps and directing my path. I ask You for divine setups and connections. Protect me from the entrapments of the enemy. In Jesus's name, amen.

13. DECLARATION

I break off every attack from the spirit of Delilah. I refuse to be manipulated, deceived, or controlled by witchcraft or any other forces of the enemy. Words or accusations of the enemy will no longer press me.

SCRIPTURE

Fear not, for I am with you; be not dismayed, for I am your God; I will strengthen you, I will help you, I will uphold you with my righteous right hand.   (Isaiah 41:10 ESV)

PRAYER

Lord, thank You for being with me. You surround me with a perfect love that casts out all fear. I command the spirit of fear to go from me now! Thank You for freeing me from accusations and lies. Every label the enemy has tried to place upon me and make me believe is cast down, as I completely surrender to You. Amen.

14. DECLARATION

My relationships and associations are ordained by the Lord. I will not connect directly or indirectly with anything or anyone who would compromise my relationship with God.

SCRIPTURE

If you want to grow in wisdom, spend time with the wise. Walk with the wicked, and you'll eventually become just like them.   (Proverbs 13:20 TPT)

PRAYER

Lord, I thank You that I hear Your voice with clarity. Help me to be quick to obey Your commands. Protect me from wrong relationships and expose every hidden spirit that would cause deception or distraction. Amen.

15. DECLARATION

I am a representative of Jesus on the earth. The Holy Spirit leads me, and I follow His voice alone. I will not be moved by circumstances, threats, or intimidation sent from the enemy.

SCRIPTURE

Then he answered and spake unto me, saying, This is the word of the LORD unto Zerubbabel, saying, Not by might, nor by power, but by my spirit, saith the LORD of hosts.

(Zechariah 4:6)

PRAYER

Lord, thank You for placing a watch upon my mouth and a guard upon my tongue, that I may speak as an oracle of the Most High God. Amen.

16. DECLARATION

I am not alone in this fight. My God is my refuge and strength. He is a very present help in the time of trouble. I will overcome every attack of the enemy.

SCRIPTURE

God is our refuge and strength, a very present help in trouble. Therefore will not we fear, though the earth be removed, and though the mountains be carried into the midst of the sea.

(Psalm 46:1–2)

PRAYER

I thank You, Lord, that You are my refuge. I ask You to give me strength and help me to remain steadfast in my faith in You. Amen.

17. DECLARATION

I am strong and courageous. I am a warrior and an overcomer. I rebuke the spirit of fear, and I stir my faith to believe You. I put my trust in Your Word. I declare that You are faithful!

SCRIPTURE

So be strong and courageous! Do not be afraid and do not panic before them. For the LORD your God will personally go ahead of you. He will neither fail you nor abandon you.
(Deuteronomy 31:6 NLT)

PRAYER

Father, I ask You to help me have strength and courage. I thank You that I can draw my power from Your unlimited supply. You empower me to defeat every attack of the enemy. Thank You for guiding me by the leading of the Holy Spirit. In Jesus' name, amen.

18. DECLARATION

I am covered by God, and He is my protector. He delivers me from the snare of the evil one. I will not be entrapped by the enemy. I will not give in to the spirit of Delilah. I will stand firm against every demonic force.

SCRIPTURE

He that dwelleth in the secret place of the most High shall abide under the shadow of the Almighty. I will say of the Lord, *He is my refuge and my fortress: my God; in him will I trust. Surely he shall deliver thee from the snare of the fowler, and from the noisome pestilence.* (Psalm 91:1–3)

PRAYER

Lord, I thank You that I can abide under Your shadow and that You are my fortress and refuge. I place my trust in You. I know that You will never fail me. Amen.

19. DECLARATION

I am the head and not the tail, above only and not beneath. I am the lender and not the borrower. I am blessed coming in and going out. I am highly favored of God and man. I am anointed for such a time as this.

SCRIPTURE

The LORD will make you the head (leader) and not the tail (follower); and you will be above only, and you will not be beneath, if you listen and pay attention to the commandments of the LORD your God, which I am commanding you today, to observe them carefully. (Deuteronomy 28:13 AMP)

PRAYER

Lord, I thank You for helping me live according to Your Word. I claim these promises over my life. I break off every distraction from my life. Help me listen and pay attention to Your commandments and walk in the fulfillment of Your promises. Amen.

20. DECLARATION

I reject every lie that is contrary to God's Word. I believe everything that He has promised is for me. I refuse to allow confusion to gain access to my mind. My purpose is clear. My hearing is tuned to His voice. My vision is focused, and I walk in God's favor.

SCRIPTURE

For as many as are the promises of God, in Christ they are [all answered] "Yes." So through Him we say our "Amen" to the glory of God.   (2 Corinthians 1:20 AMP)

PRAYER

Father, thank You for answering "yes" to every promise. I come into agreement with Your Word and say, "Amen" (so be it). I believe today that every word You have spoken is coming forth in my life. I thank You that You will receive glory from the way You are moving for me. I am a testimony of Your power. Amen!

ABOUT THE AUTHOR

Andrew Towe is an emerging prophetic voice to this generation. His bold delivery and explosive preaching are authenticated by his accuracy, integrity, and passion for seeing lives transformed by the power of God.

Andrew's words and ministry are earmarked by the weight of God's glory. He actively demonstrates God's power by flowing in the gifts of the Spirit and prophetically declaring the Word of God.

The message of awakening and revival are threaded throughout Andrew's life and his voice of ministry. His meetings are saturated with the manifested presence of God.

Andrew and his wife, Brooke, reside with their two children reside in Chattanooga, Tennessee, and are the lead pastors of Ramp Church Chattanooga. They are under the covering of The Ramp in Hamilton, Alabama.

As a writer, Andrew releases prophetic words often published on The Elijah List, in *Charisma Magazine*, and in other publications. His book *The Triple Threat Anointing,* published by Destiny Image, was released in October 2020 and was a No. 1 New Release in two of its categories on Amazon.

Andrew's podcast, *Dynamic Fire,* is available on Apple and Spotify and is featured on the Destiny Image Podcast Network.

Andrew is also an international conference speaker. He has been featured on various prominent broadcasts on Christian television networks including *Sid Roth's It's Supernatural!* and TBN's flagship program, *Praise.* He has ministered on Trinity Broadcasting Network, Christian Television Network, and Tri-State Christian Television.

Andrew is aggressively building the kingdom of God and releasing the prophetic Word of God through leading his local church, writing, and speaking.